Podger's Farm

Michael H. Power

Pen Press

First published in Great Britain by Pen Press

All paper used in the printing of this book has been made from wood
grown in managed, sustainable forests.

ISBN 13: 978-1-907172-07-6

Printed and bound in the UK
Pen Press is an imprint of Indepenpress Publishing Limited
25 Eastern Place
Brighton
BN2 1GJ

A catalogue record of this book is available from
the British Library

Cover design by Jacqueline Abromeit

(Left to right) Back row: Kenny Harding, Carl Jones, Skally Plant
Front row: Mary, Bill, Me

Pictures by kind permission of Colin (Masso) Bird

Bill, Me, Bob the dog and Skally Plant

Chapter One

My first memory is of the sun shining through a window. I was a toddler before I recall anything else.

My parents and grandparents had moved from New Mills farm where I had been born. New Mills was about half-a-mile south of Walsall town and surrounded by urban development with only the house, a couple of barns and a few pigsties left of the original farm. Bescot farm where we now lived was a much bigger farm on the south-west edge of Walsall borough on its border with Darlaston and Wednesbury. Although its name was Bescot farm it was always referred to as Podger's farm by all our friends, 'Podger' being the nickname I was usually known by at school.

My first recollection was pulling a little cart round the yard and peddling a car along the top landing of the large farmhouse. I have no memory at this time of my brother and sister who were twins; Malcolm (who everyone called Bill) and Mary, although I do remember my mother's Old English Sheepdog called Biddie.

I have a vague memory of an outing probably about 1935 and I think the trip was a day out in Sutton Park. I was togged out in a knitted romper suit and recall getting stuck in some brambles. The knitted romper suit must have been our standard dress as both my mother and her mother were keen knitters; in fact one of their romper suits was the cause of my brother Bill going missing. It was a bright summer's morning when everyone realised Bill was missing and the search was on. There was an old sandpit in the top field and everyone thought he may have gone down there to play, but a search failed to find him. Then someone heard crying and going in that direction they found Bill; he had crawled across the field, down a bank towards the pool and tried to go under a barbed wire fence. The bottom strand of the wire had got caught in his romper suit and left Bill hanging there. Luckily he hadn't hurt himself and was no worse for his little adventure.

About the same time as Bill had got stuck on the barbed wire Tom Perry (a butcher in the Pleck) had dumped an old nanny goat on my dad. They were planning to keep it as a pet for us kids and tied it to the apple tree in the garden. I well remember them trying to introduce me to it, but I was terrified of the thing. I don't remember whatever became of the goat.

The farm fields extended to about 44 acres and were divided into three fields. One large field ran from the railway by Pleck Park to the Darlaston Road. It had a pool fed by a stream and was separated from the top fields by a ditch. A path ran along the edge from the Darlaston Road to Pleck Park.

One morning our Grandmother Bertha took us for a walk. She looked after us kids as our mother was always working. It must have been in the springtime as the ditches only filled with water when we had a lot of wet weather. Like all little boys, I thought it would be great fun to throw stones into the water. Dire warnings from my Granny didn't stop me and the next thing I was in the water. Even now, if I close my eyes I can still see how green it was under the water. The whole episode resulted in much laughter from my brother and sister and a good thumping for me.

My father used to show Large White pigs and in the late summer this would result in a trip to Bearwood Show. It must have been my first trip there and I can't recall much about it except for a lorry with a model of a large brown bottle on it (probably an advert for beer), and also some men flying through the air on motorbikes. I don't remember if my dad won any prizes, but I think this was the last time he showed any pigs until he put a pen of four Porkers in the 1938 Wolverhampton Christmas Fat Stock Sales and won first prize; fifteen shillings and a brass plate that I still have. The story was that my father had taken them in with the purpose of getting the money to pay the rent on the farm, due on Christmas Day. Winning first prize, he got top whack for the pigs in the sale, and fifteen bob as well.

My mother was always very busy on Saturday as her plan for making money was selling clothes from a Littlewoods catalogue. Her transport for this was a 'sit-up and beg' bicycle with a little sidecar on it. How she had enough breath to pedal it with all the fags she smoked (eighty a day) I will never know. She had customers all over Walsall, but her main customers were in the slums around

St Matthew's Church. Generally, the families were very large and lived in small two-up, two-down houses that were usually in poor repair. At this time the council had started to clear some of the slums and was moving people to the Delves where they were building new houses even though half of them couldn't pay the rent on the old houses.

Of the few times I went with my mother to the old town, my strongest memory is of the smell of the place, it smelt a bit high particularly in the summer all around Church Hill, Birmingham Street and Peal Street. A lot of the housing was very old single brick and of poor quality. Most families who lived in this area were unemployed or 'on the Parish' as it was called. A child's vest probably cost ten pence or a shilling, so they would buy clothes on the 'weekly' or the 'glad and sorry' as some called it. Sales were always good; getting the money off them was the main problem.

Of the large families I remember are the Crutchleys who lived in Caldmore; Mrs Horny who lived near the Quarry at Bentley and Mrs Davis who lived in Lord Street, Palfrey. I think one of Mrs Davis' daughters had my sister Mary as a bridesmaid at her wedding. I remember we all went to a bun-struggle after the wedding that was held at the Tin Tabernacle in Sun Street.

My mother certainly got about the town on her bike but by the late 1930s things had started to change. The threat of War was in the air and industry was picking up. Men who had been out of work for most of the last decade were getting jobs and becoming more affluent. Hence, the need to buy things on the 'glad and sorry' started to vanish, although I well remember my mother going round until early 1941 collecting the money still owed to her.

Easter 1937 and time for me to get an education. I was four years old when my mother took me to Hilary Street School. My granny, who used to take me around, must have been left to look after Bill and Mary that day. We were met at the entrance by the headmistress and taken to the nursery class to meet the teacher Miss James. She was a tall, grey-haired lady dressed in a Queen Victoria surplus dress and button boots; there was going to be no messing with her. And so it proved to be. The classroom was fairly large; it had two rows of desks and on the left side there was a play area with a wooden sandpit. You had to take turns in the sandpit, as it was always over-subscribed at playtime. We were put to sit in a double row of little desks that had cast iron frames with wooden seats and lift up lids. We were placed two to a desk in two rows; girls in one row, boys in another. I was sat next to a lad named Joey Fox who lived in Queen Street. Most of the class settled down after the parents left but one little chap, Ronnie Ridding kept trying to escape. After several attempts he was sat between Joey and me and we were charged to keep Ronnie captive while proceedings went on. Ronnie soon settled in.

The school day was from nine o'clock in the morning until twelve noon with a two-hour lunch. At ten thirty we had a break of fifteen minutes in the school playground. The afternoon session was from two until three, although this went to four thirty after our first year. We started our day with names from the register to which we answered 'yes miss' then followed the Miss James nose blowing ritual. We all got out our hankies (or bit of rag for most of us) and blew our noses; woe betide any one without a rag as Miss James would make us use a strip of newspaper – very hard on tender young noses. Prayers followed, where we learned our first hymn and the only one I remember; 'All Things Bright and Beautiful'.

We each had little slates in a wooden frame and a stick of French chalk on which we learned to form letters and numbers. At playtime, a small bottle of milk was given free to all of the class whose fathers were on the 'Parish'. If your Dad had a job, it was two pence halfpenny a week. In the afternoon we would have half an hour painting or playing with plasticine, then little mats were placed in the clear end of the classroom and we would lie down until home time. I never liked this as I always imagined there was a giant rat looking at us through the large window at the end of the classroom. One day, on my way home for lunch, Miss James caught me having a wee in a gateway in Hilary Street. When I returned to school she had me in front of the class and made it quite plain what sort of animal she thought I was. She then marched me across the playground and shut me in the little outhouse where the caretaker kept his sawdust. I was probably only in there for half an hour, but it seemed a lot longer. I was too terrified to cry, it was pitch dark in there and it made me afraid of the dark for years after.

Relief was to come in September when Miss James was replaced by a Miss Wood, and with a young teacher things took a turn for the better, Miss Wood was a lot easier on us kids.

The highlights of the year 1937 for me were the coronation and a holiday at Rhyl. The holiday I do not remember much about except for the smell of the sea and being in a room where you could hear it but couldn't see it.

The coronation I remember more. Our first day off school was for the coronation of George V1, for which we had all been given a lead medal with a red, white and blue ribbon. We joined the Dora Street party that was held on a little field that ran between Dora Street and Kingsley Street, probably because most of my mother's friends lived in Dora Street. We had cake and jelly, and my mother made the ice-cream for the event, which was done with a machine from the shop she and Granny used to have in Palfrey. This was a large wooden bucket with a metal container in the middle, with a paddle turned by a geared handle on the top. Ice-cream was made by putting a gallon of custard in the metal container, packing the wooden bucket with ice and turning the handle for an hour. Afterwards there were games and we all had a great time.

At the start of the next school year my brother and sister would join me. Being born before Easter 1933, I would leave school at age fourteen. Because they were younger than me and born after Easter 1933, they would be the first year to leave school at fifteen.

I think I was allowed to come home from school on my own. The usual route was down Hilary Street, along Wallows Lane, down Mountford Drive and through Pleck Park. Bill and I came that way one hot summer's day and stopped to play on the slide in the park until we were sent off by some posh woman with two kids. They were not going to share the slide with scruffy little guttersnipes like Bill and me. Bill found a stick and dipped it in some tar that the sun had melted on the path, and daubed it on the slide – that buggered them up!

Although going home through the park was our main route, we would sometimes come up over the Brown Lion and then we could go down Kingsley Street, or turn down Bescot Road and along Slater's Lane. It was coming home this way that comes to mind if I think of my father. We were running in and out of the shrubs on the

Brown Lion island one afternoon when I heard his voice and there he was. He had been to kill and dress some lambs for Franz Shumaker, a German Butcher in Palfrey. Dad was a butcher by trade and was noted for killing and dressing lambs, so he made a bit of extra money doing it, Denham's in Caldmore was another butcher he would occasionally kill and dress lambs for as well.

It was now 1938 and I was in my second year at school. We were in the big-time now; we had left our slates in the nursery class and Miss Cowley was the teacher.

Our first major project was Empire Day and we used crayons to make little Union Jacks out of paper. A map of the world was pinned on the blackboard and all the red bits pointed out to us – 'The Great British Empire' over which our beloved King ruled. We English were number one, all the rest were happy little natives dancing in the sun. We marched around the playground waving our Union Jacks singing 'Flag of our Empire' then I think we finished school early.

There were lots of distractions on our way to and from school; Ernie Heath's Coachworks in Hilary Street was one. They made and repaired milk floats and horse-drawn carts etc; the interesting bit was when they were making wooden wheels and would get the iron rims hot to shrink onto the wood. The wheel used to groan as the band cooled on it.

Norman Round's Smithy at the bottom of Wellington Street was another. You could always have a good half hour watching him. He didn't buy horse shoes ready made like they do today; he made his own out of a bar of steel. Most deliveries were made by horse and cart – bread, milk and coal – all before the days of fetch your own.

The park way was always our favourite way home and we had many happy hours in there before slipping through the fence into the farmyard for our tea. About six thirty a small zinc bath was placed on the kitchen table, filled with hot water from the kettles off the hob and the three of us would get scrubbed ready for bed. We liked our mother to do it, as Granny McClement was a bit heavy-handed.

Bill would never go to bed without a scruffy little Bear with no legs called Noorky. He was always losing it in the yard but it would have to be found before you could get Bill to bed.

We went to Blackpool for our summer holidays which took some preparation. The packing was done a few days before the holiday; everything needed, including our knitted bathing costumes (cozers), was packed into a wicker hamper about thirty inches by twenty and two feet deep with a canvas cover. This would be fetched by the railway carter a couple of days before we were due to go and sent on ahead so it would be at our holiday digs when we arrived.

On the great day we would walk to Pleck station and get the train to Wolverhampton. There we caught a train north, we may have had to change again at Crewe, then on to Blackpool for our holiday with Mother and Granny McClements. Dad was left to look after the farm. We must have had good weather because I remember spending a lot of time on the beach and having donkey rides, but our best day was a boat trip. We were taken off the beach on a small boat out to *The Girl Pat*, a fishing boat that had been made famous in 1935 when it had been stolen from Grimsby by a George Orsbourn and his mate. They had sailed it down the coast of Spain and Africa, gun running or something like that, and then sailed to South America. Now the owners were making a quick bob or two doing trips with it. Here we were, Mom, Granny and us three kids out on the ocean, well the Irish Sea; the first sea trip for us kids. Being British it's our heritage isn't it? It may not compare with the exploits of Drake or Nelson but we kids enjoyed it.

Another highlight was going to a concert, where I think the singer may have been the Australian Peter Dawson. I was not impressed with his singing. I do recall a demonstration we were given on a pressure cooker; a big aluminium thing. Mother bought one and sent it home, Dad thought it was a bomb when it arrived and put it in the corner of one of the barns. Mother was not best pleased when we got back home as some of the fowl had crapped on it.

It was a good year as we kids played around the farmyard. Me, being my granny's favourite, would sometimes go up to the room on the second floor where she lived with old Mac her husband. He had spent most of his life at sea but was now retired and he would spend most of his days down Walsall Station carrying the passengers' bags to the taxi rank for a few coppers, until he had enough money for a couple of pints in The Brown Lion on his way home. The room was very large and the fireplace stood well out leaving an inglenook each side. The bed was on one side and a large cupboard in the other. I spent many happy hours up there looking out of the window. You could see all across the park and the fields beyond, all the way up to the top of Wednesbury. You could hear F. H. Lloyds Brass Band practising in the sports pavilion on summer nights. Watching the express trains thunder along the line on the far side of the Park on their way north was another pleasure. This came to an end later in the year when Granddad had a stroke and they moved to a room downstairs at the front of the house. It was no more carrying bags for old Mac. He ended up in a wheelchair.

It was about this time I got into pinching matches and started a fire or two. I don't think I did much damage; setting fire to the wheel of Bob James' cart was my only success, however a thumping and being locked in the bedroom for the day proved to be a cure for my fire-raising ambitions. The same cure was used when I got into pinching money and going to Selves shop in Dora Street and buying sweets.

When the weather was good in the summer, Granny would walk us up to Wednesbury Park for the afternoon where there was a paddling pool. We had great fun in it with our knitted cozers on. Sometimes (not very often) we would get an ice-cream from the Midland Counties man on his three-wheeled bike with a box on the front. Most times it would be two ice-creams, cut in half between the four of us. Going to the 'Arbo' (the Arboretum is Walsall's major park) was another trip. We would catch the inner circle bus by the Brown lion and go all round the Broadway to the Arbo. Fishing for 'bullheads' in the little stream was the main attraction there. We had many happy hours.

Pleck Park was our main playground, well it was next to the farm – just through the fence and over the railway bridge; it had swings, a slide, a roundabout and a great thing called the giant-stride and everyone went on that. At the back of the park (we called the Rookery) was the remains of Bescot Hall. Most of it had vanished but there were still odd bits left like the moat and an arched wall and a little stream that ran down towards the railway.

At the bottom end of the park was a pool known to us kids as 'the Bog' that had formed in the depression where two railway lines met.

Next to the farm was an area that was originally part of Pleck Park. It had later been a sandpit but was now used as a tip, although the original park paths were still around it. Some of the out-of-work families like the Lees and the Dykes and a character who we called Old Foy (whom we kids were always scared of) would spend their days raking it over for the scrap metal which they sold to Sid Lewis the coal merchant.

It was on one bright summer's day in this part of the park we met a man who we knew as his son was in my class at school. He took us down the railway bank and then exposed himself. We kids ran off home and told our mother and a lady came to interview us a couple of days later, but after that we heard no more of it. We soon forgot about it (the 'scarred for life idea' had not been invented yet) and I can't remember what happened to the man but we still saw him around the park. I think the Police may have just given him a warning.

When we were not in the park we would be playing around the farmyard or in what we called the garden. This was the area in front of the house that had been a nice garden once but was now overgrown with horseradish. It had an apple and a pear tree, although the best pear trees were on the far end of the house and there was another at the end of a barn by the field. The garden was separated by a hedge of hazel and lilac from what looked like a large lawn with an ornamental wall in front. We called this the 'Pig Field' because Dad used to let the young pigs have a run on it when he cleaned out their sty.

When the weather was poor we would play around the house; a large three-storey building with massive rooms. The large room next to the kitchen we called the scullery and Mother did the washing in there. I remember a large rocking horse in this room on which we had hours of fun.

We were allowed to play in the top rooms that were not in use. There were four-poster beds in two of the four rooms. We would ride our bikes up there and have a high old time until we fell out with one another, then I would run to Granny and complain about them two kids. There were another four bedrooms on the second floor; all large, Mom and Dad slept in the front overlooking the park, we kids were on the side of the house overlooking the fields.

The view from the windows up there was great as you could see for miles The view of Darlaston was blocked by F. H. Lloyds, but you could see Wednesbury and Stone Cross and all the factories along Darlaston Green. It was good on dark nights when they would run the molten iron off and the sky would glow but it was even better if we had low cloud to reflect it.

As the year progressed Old Mac got a little better and we would sit on his bed while he told us stories of his time at sea. He even showed us how to put a three-masted ship about in stormy weather, which kept him happy until his tales got a bit too tall. Granny got him a wheelchair (well it was more like an adult pushchair) so he got out a bit. He also had a little battery-powered machine that gave an electric shock, you held it in your hands and it was supposed to help rheumatism.

Chapter Two

One morning in early summer 1938 there was a crowd in the field by Darlaston Road so we all ran up to see what was happening. A small double-winged plane had landed on the field; they had dropped in to pay a visit to Rubery Owens who owned a large factory in Darlaston. There was great excitement as none of us had ever been near a plane before. It was all people talked about for weeks after.

It was a good job it didn't land in the first field as Dad was keeping that for hay and it was about ready for cutting. This would be another fun time for us kids. Dad borrowed a mower off someone and put Bonnie his old mare in the shafts; it took all day until nine o'clock in the evening to cut it all and poor old Bonnie was knackered by the end of it. The hay was then left for a couple of days to dry out. Another job for old Bonnie was the hay rake that drew the hay up into ridges across the field. We kids were now roped in to help to pile the hay up into little stooks ready to be loaded on to the cart. This was a memorable time for me as Dad taught me to drive a horse and cart while we where collecting the hay, it's never been any use to me but at least I know how.

Dad would sometimes take us with him when he went out with the horse and float. He would go two or three times a week to the General Hospital where he collected the kitchen waste for pig food which he had to boil. It always had a couple of spoons, knives or forks left in the waste but it kept us and a few other people in cutlery. Another place we would go for waste was the Co-Op Bakery in Shaw Street. This was mainly floor sweepings but it helped feed the pigs and we liked to go there as the foreman baker would give us kids a new loaf which we would eat on our way home. We used to end up with the 'todd' through eating too much, but we loved it. Stanley's the corn merchant was another trip, they wholesaled groceries as well. They had a place in Bridge Street and we would fetch pig meal and fowl corn from there.

September saw us back at school with me in my last year of the infants and Bill and Mary in their second year of three. My teacher was now a Miss Edwards who kept her moth-eaten old fur coat on in the classroom summer and winter. It was in this class I first remember the nit nurse who came to check us for nits. It was supposed to be very confidential but we all knew who had the nits as they were called out to the front of the class and given a letter at home time. Another little game was the shoe inspection for the kids whose fathers were on the Parish. If, in the opinion of the head-teacher their footwear was not suitable for the winter they would be given a note to take to Hewitt's shoe shop at the bottom of Stafford Street. Here they would get fitted up with a pair of boots, with an embossed stamp on the ankle to stop their parents pawning them. The boots were paid for out of The Lord Mayor's Shoe Fund, but I don't suppose the Mayor ever put his hand in his pocket to pay for any of them.

It was about this time we were met from school by Mother and Granny and taken to the Picture House on the Bridge to see *Snow White and the Seven Dwarfs*. We nearly wet ourselves with excitement until the film got going. When the wicked witch came on it terrified Bill and he hid under the seats. Mother had a job to get him out, however Mary and I thought it was great, as we had never seen a film before.

We had another adventure about this time; Mother took us to Pat Collins' fair for a treat. There we met our Aunty Sarah, one of Dad's sisters, with her youngest son Gordon (one of our cousins) who came home with us with a view of spending a few days down on the farm. Mary may have gone back with Aunt Sarah as all her children were boys and she used to have Mary for a few days sometimes. All went well until bedtime when we were all put to bed in the same large room. This had a fireplace that jutted out into the room with a nook each side big enough to hold a bed. Gordon was put in a bed by the far wall and we settled down for the night until Gordon complained he was cold. Bill and I, being helpful and wanting to make Gordon's stay with us comfortable, lit some candles under his bed to warm him up a bit. The resulting fire was soon put out but Gordy lost his appetite for farming and had to be taken home. All the thanks we got was a thumping − we never found out if it was for lighting the candles or for pinching the matches to light them.

Life went on, Mother still out with her bike and sidecar on Saturdays trying to make her fortune and Dad doing the pigs and moving the odd load of furniture with his cart. He had a couple of helpers; Harry Bagnal a big man with rheumatic lumps on his hands and arms who had holes cut in his boots for the lumps on his feet to stick out and Dickey Colley who only came when he didn't have a job. They worked for a bit of dinner and enough money to get a couple of pints on their way home at night.

We kids decided to let 1938 out with a bang so we all had the Measles. This altered our sleeping arrangements so I spent the nights in Mac and Granny's room and Bill and Mary with Mother. I slept on a chair that folded down into a bed that was placed by the fire, an open fire with a basket. The itching was a nightmare and I could have scratched my skin off. Starch was supposed to be the relief but it never seemed to work. I was still there when Santa came and he brought us cowboy suits that year: hat, belt and guns had been bought but the rest had been codged up by Mother, like the waistcoats and trousers.

Mother was Mac and Bertha's only child, but Dad came from a family of eight, four girls who were all older than the four boys. His father, George Power M.B.E., could best be described as a man's man or, as most of his daughters-in-law called him, an old pig. My mother always reckoned he had got the M.B.E. for scrounging beer and watching his antics in The Swan at Fradley gave us no reason to doubt this. His wife Granny Power was a big woman, she never said much though she would make two of George. Always eating, she loved picking the meat off bones.

Their eldest child was our aunt Dora. She was a slim elegant lady who lived with her second husband in West Bromwich Street. She had two children, Jeffrey and Barbara who both had kids of their own. Aunt Dora always had her smelling salts with her as she was given to attacks of the vapours. She was also a J.P. but how she managed when she was on the bench in court, God knows.

The second eldest was Nellie who lived at Kettering in Northamptonshire. We only met her a couple of times; she was a big lady like Granny Power. Percy her husband we would see more often as he worked in the shoe trade and would come up with boots for us. They had a daughter Kathy, but I only remember seeing her once.

Sarah was their third daughter. She lived at Shelfield with her husband Bill Taylor known by all as Busty; he loved a party and always appointed himself in charge of proceedings. They had five sons: Bill, Ron, Douglas, Ken and Gordon. Sarah was Dad's favourite sister. He and his brother Albert had lived with Sarah for a while when she had her butcher's shop in West Bromwich Street. Their father would come home boozed-up some nights and set about their Mother. Dad and Albert went down the stairs one night while he was setting about her and threatened to thump their dad if he didn't stop belting their mother. Their father threw them out and they had to camp out with Sarah and Busty.

The youngest daughter was Kate. She was a widow with two sons Austin and Neil. Her husband died in 1939. She had a shop in Leamore which I remember visiting once with my Granny. That was all Dad's sisters.

Of Dad's brothers, George (the eldest) lived in Tame Street just up from his parents. He was married to Maud and had four children, Ronald, Doris (the eldest), Sheila and Audrey. Uncle George and Aunty Maud were always kind to us kids, with a couple of biscuits or three pence to spend when we visited them and Uncle George would come to the farm most Saturdays.

Albert was the next son. He was married to a French lady, Rene. They had one son, Trevor who was the same age as me. Albert had a Haberdashery shop in Caldmore. I think his wife had started it before she opened a school. Albert had also taken over a hat shop from Granddad Power's sister Sarah in George Street but spent most of his time running around in his car wholesaling anything he could make a few bob on. Dad always called him our Punka, Dad and Albert were as thick as thieves. Aunty Rene ran a school grandly called St Georges Academy on the Wednesbury Road. This was known in later years for turning out works secretaries.

Harry, our father was only about twelve months younger than Albert so that's probably why they were so close.

Gabriel was the youngest by a few years; he lived down the Delves with his wife Gwen and two children John and Valerie. Gabriel was in the leather industry like his father had been and it would be a few years before he had his own firm 'The Walsall Riding Saddle and Gabriel Power Ltd'.

All the boys except George had their own businesses; Albert haberdashery, Harry farming, Gabe leather. Two of the girls also; Sarah was a butcher and Kate sold second-hand clothes.

My Dad and his father had obviously made up their differences with Granddad Power as he was a regular visitor to the farm, if it was only to scrounge a few eggs. He was well known around Walsall for his work in the Labour movement. He had been secretary of The Midland Leather Trades Federation and was their life President. He had founded the Walsall Brown Saddlers Protection Society as a young man and in July 1910, along with fellow leather workers, formed The Amalgamated Society of Harness Makers Bridle Cutters and Fancy Leather Workers in the Prince Blucher Pub in Stafford Street. He was secretary of this union. During The First World War he was also on the Leather Supplies Advisory Committee and this was probably why he was awarded his M.B.E. George was a trustee of The Leather Workers' Pension Fund and a Poor Law Guardian. With all this and working a 54-hour week I don't know how he found time to have eight kids.

Mother being an only child only had uncles and aunts. Her dad Mac (William MacClements) had two brothers, both seamen like he had been though they lived in Hamilton, Scotland.

His wife Bertha, Mother's mother was one of six; three brothers and three sisters and came from Wellsbourne in Warwickshire. Her eldest brother Fred lived in Sutton with his wife Nan, who we kids always called Aunty Nan. They had a son whose name I can't recall. Granny would often take us to visit them and they were regular visitors to us. Charlie Clarke, another brother, lived with his wife and daughter at Stoke-on-Trent. I remember going on the train to visit them once. I don't know what had happened between Bertha and her youngest brother Steven but he was never mentioned.

Of the two sisters Millicent and Adelaide, one lived in Manchester, and the other who was blind lived in Devon. Granny would go and spend some time with both of them during the summer and take our sister Mary with her. Mary would always come home speaking the accent of the area they had been to visit.

There were always people about the farmyard at this time in 1939. Dad didn't have any cows and let the fields out for grazing. This was used by several of the coal wharfs that would give their big carthorses a couple of days' rest occasionally. They needed it most of them, they were often asleep while standing.

15

A couple of hawkers, Sid Perrins and Bob James turned their horses out at night after they had finished and they kept us in fruit and vegetables so we did all right. It was Sid Perrins' generosity that caused me to clonk our Mary on the head with a hammer. Sid had left us kids an apple each in a barrel on his cart but Mary decided she was having the apples herself and had climbed into the barrel to stop Bill and me getting one. She wouldn't come out of the barrel so I hit her on the head with a hammer – that got her out but there was blood everywhere. Dad grabbed Mary and ran down to Dr Davis with her. Fortunately it wasn't as bad as it looked and Mary only needed one stitch. Bill always reckoned our Mary was never right in the head after that.

Another memorable character was old Boffy who was a boatman, he owned a big white mule he used for pulling barges. This mule went for me once when I was in the field and I was lucky one of my older cousins Jeff Slater was behind me and threw a brick which hit the mule on the head stopping it in its tracks. When the ostlers came to fetch the working horses back, the horses knew they were going back to work, so there were always problems trying to catch them but they would get them in the end after herding them into a corner.

There was also a little riding pony belonging to the Ingram family. They let us kids ride it and we even had our photos taken on it wearing our cowboy rig-outs, which Mother had framed and hung on the living room wall.

Sunday mornings people would come to check their horses and was always the time for putting the world to rights; there was a lot of yapping went on until the pubs opened. Tom Perry would came to do a bit of shooting on the pool and fields with his old twelve bore shot-gun although he never shot anything. Mother used to say the safest place was to have Tom aiming at you.

It was about this time we got roped in for attending Sunday school. A Mr Yard, who was warden at St John's church, had seen Granny Mac. She was a regular churchgoer and used to take Mary with her when she went. Now it was time to round Bill and me up and it was months before we escaped. I think the man taking the class was called-up for the army so we were saved by providence.

Dad started to acquire some day-old calves. A couple at a time, these little animals still had to be fed on milk. This came in powder form in cardboard barrels and was mixed with water; we kids thought it great fun feeding them until the novelty wore off. The milk was put in a bucket and you put your hand in the milk and stuck two fingers out so the calf would suck them and this way the calf learned to drink out of the bucket. This went on for about six weeks and by then they would be on solid food and grazing. The calves would then be put in a little field at the end of the lane that led to the farm. This we called the Meadow and had two raised circles in it, each about twenty feet in diameter that showed it had once been a rickyard. After a few weeks in the meadow they were sent to Barwells who had a farm on Barr Beacon. The grazing was much better there and we would visit them from time to time. Dad got his first six cows this way, but it would be another two years before they calved and gave milk.

Things must have got better in farming and Mother was determined to improve our image. The room Mac and Bertha had lived in was all papered and done out as it was the only upstairs room with a gas light in. New furniture was bought from Jays in Digbeth, a fancy three-piece suite plus a large carpet and the must-have of all social climbing families, a piano, although we kids would later come to regret the purchase of this item. The room was now called The Drawing Room, very posh, but we kids were of course barred, though we were allowed a Christmas Party in it with some of our school friends.

We didn't get to go to the sea-side this year, our highlight was a trip to Dudley Zoo; well we had to, King George had only officially opened it last year and he had even had a ride on the miniature steam-train.

We went on the train, the Dudley Dasher as it was always known from Walsall station and it only went to Dudley, the line ending by the Zoo. It was pulled by a little tank engine with a tall chimney. When I remember this trip the first thing that comes to mind is the penguins in their pool, it had a little tunnel you could go in to watch them swimming under water. I was very impressed. I was also very much taken with the polar bear. The elephants were giving rides when we got round to them but only Mary and I had one. As soon as Bill saw the elephant he was off like a ferret up a drain-pipe – this was a surprise as Bill always had an affection for animals; he could get them to do anything even as a kid. Bill always reckoned the elephant rolled its eyes at him so Granny took him down the pets corner while Mary and I had a ride. Mother had brought a large bag of sandwiches with her and we had our lunch in the Pets Corner, this rivalled the Chimps tea-party which we went to see later. The day was rounded off by a ride on the miniature train – well if it's good enough for the King it's good enough for us! Back to Walsall on the Dudley Dasher; we had had a great day.

We arrived back home to find Dad had got a new yard dog that Dickey Colley had brought him. Dickey had got a job driving a lorry collecting from the docks and delivering to warehouses. One of the warehouse guard dogs had got loose and jumped in the back of Dickey's lorry and nobody could get him out again, so Dickey had brought him to Dad; he got the dog out of the lorry and he was put in a stall in the stable. He was a big crossbred animal that we called Joey and he had a head like a bucket He soon got used to us all but he was nasty with anyone he didn't know so he was kept in the stall during the day and let out to roam the yard at night along with Dad's little terrier, Mick.

As the year wore on all the talk was of war and the Sunday morning yard conferences got more intense. As far as we kids could make out it was all the fault of the Balkans, and someone called Hitler. A lot of the young men had already been called up to the forces, some of our older cousins and Uncle Gabe had gone and although war had not yet been declared, preparations were being made. All households were issued with an Anderson air-raid shelter with instructions to bury it for half its depth in the garden and put the dug-out soil on top. Dad and Harry Bagnal made a start on doing ours but it was abandoned when Mother said she wouldn't be running across the garden in the middle of the night to get to it for nobody, so we set up camp in the cellar. This was large, and had a wall down the middle making it into two rooms, so our beds were set up on the sill of the right-hand cellar and the place was turned into a comfortable little bolt-hole for the coming air-raids.

Preparations went on apace; now when Dad fetched pig meal from Stanley's he was bringing boxes of tinned food as well, these together with eggs put down in isinglass (a preservative) was stored in the cupboard in the drawing room. A padlock was put on the door, which I think was just to keep out the German spies who the newspapers kept telling us where everywhere. A new wireless was bought, well a nearly new one from Dad's brother Albert. As we had no electricity on the farm it was a battery set with valves in it that lit up when it was working. It required a battery the size of two house bricks and an accumulator that had to be charged which was done at Southalls the ironmongers.

We all gathered round the wireless in September 1939 to hear a statement by Neville Chamberlain the Prime Minister, the gist being Neville had written to Adolph Hitler telling him to stop his antics in Poland or else. Adolph had written back, telling Nev to get stuffed, so Nev blew the whistle to start the Second World War.

It may have been the shock of this, I will never know, but old Mac died in October. We kids were spared his funeral and taken to stay for the day with Mrs Smith, one of Mother's friends who lived in Dora St, but we did get to meet Mac's two brothers, kindly old Scotsmen, who gave us kids a half-crown each.

Granny met us from school one afternoon and we were taken to a little church hall on the corner of Caledon Street to be fitted with gas masks. These came in strong cardboard boxes with a string on so we could carry them over our shoulder but Granny made us leatherette cases to put them in. For the next few weeks, our first thing at school in the mornings was gas mask drill – until the novelty wore off.

Chapter Three

It was autumn 1939 and the civil defence was set up in one of the big houses on the Bescot Road. This was turned into an N.F.S. fire station complete with home-made fire engines and ambulances, which had been made out of large cars with their backs cut off. 'Commandeered off people for the duration' was the expression used to justify this robbery by the government.

The A.R.P. was set up, volunteers were given navy blue uniforms and tin helmets and some streets had a little hut together with buckets of sand and water, extension ladders and a stirrup pump. The men were called air-raid wardens and as there was a total blackout, they would patrol the streets at night to check no one had a light showing.

Air-raid shelters were built on the tip, one at the bottom of Gower Street and one in Dora Street. Two large water tanks where installed, one in Mountford Drive and the other at the Brown Lion.

Dad was not too pleased when a man with a bulldozer arrived one morning. He dug a trench across the middle of the fields that was supposed to stop German planes landing on it. The army came a couple of weeks later and they built two large huts on the top field and set up camp with a search-light and a machine gun on a stick.

Our parents were not too happy about it although they later became friends with a lot of the men but we kids thought it all great fun. Flanagan and Allen sang 'we're going to hang out the washing on the Siegfried Line', barrage balloons went up around Brum, and we slid towards 1940.

I was in the junior school now with a Miss Austin teaching. She had come to Hillary Street from Shelfield School where she had taught my cousin Gordon so I hoped there was scope to do a bit of creeping, but there never was. There were a couple of new faces in the class, they were evacuees sent from the London area to escape the bombing They spoke with funny accents but we soon taught them to talk proper.

I was struggling with my schoolwork, particularly with my reading and writing, so my Granny took me in hand. A book called

Bonzo the Dog was found; it was all about the adventures of a little fat dog and I would have to read this for half-an-hour every night under her instruction. I never looked forward to it and I would sooner have been with Bill and Mary helping Mother bodge a rug, and although my reading got much better I never learnt to spell very well.

My moment came when we had a lesson on the natives of Borneo, or somewhere like that, and we were asked to make a model of one of their houses on stilts, for homework. I got some straw off Dad and glued it to card in lengths so it looked like Bamboo to make a little hut and cut strips of green paper for the roof. When I took it to school the next day I'd hit the jackpot. I got twelve out of ten and a gold star, I was king of the class for a day and I even had kids from the next class in to view my handiwork.

It was the week before the Christmas holidays and the last couple of days would be spent in the school hall where each class would do a little play or provide some entertainment. The class creepers took full advantage of this opportunity to go for the starring roles so there were a lot of disappointments. Poor readers and writers need not apply, so that cut half the class out for a start, however we had a good couple of days before we broke-up.

We had a Christmas Party to which most of our school friends came; this was held in our posh room. We were not allowed to eat in there, the cake and jelly was served on the kitchen table together with the drinks. It was a pity no one could play our new piano, but there was a large wind-up gramophone with Granny's old records, so we played a few of them. Mother organised games and we sang carols, we were even allowed to pull crackers in there. Time was called about seven thirty and it had been great party, we only had to wait for Santa to come now. When he did he brought me a Meccano set, (a second-hand one – well there was a war on). Our main treat this Christmas was a trip to the pantomime at Wednesbury Hippodrome on Boxing Day. Mother even bought us a tub of ice-cream during the interval. What we didn't know then was this would be the last ice-cream we would have until well after the end of the war.

Although we had been at war since September, nothing seemed to be happening. Although they were building shelters and things, no one seemed to be shooting.

1940 started with us being issued ration books in January, covering a few items to start such as butter and sugar. Most other foods, with the exception of bread and vegetables were added over the next few months. When sugar went on ration, so did sweets and we were allowed two ounces a week but this didn't last very long and after a couple of months there was none to be had anyway. You had to be content with a halfpenny slice of Swede from Stantons' fish shop if you wanted something to chew. With rationing, you no longer could just buy your groceries from any shop, you had to register with a grocer – Parkers at the top of Kingsley Street was ours. As we produced our own eggs we registered with ourselves for these. Mother still went to Sissies in Dora Street for her bits and pieces that were not rationed.

The Ministry of Agriculture sent an inspector from Stafford to count all Dad's pigs and he would have to keep a record of how many piglets the sows farrowed, and dates of the ones sent for slaughter. There was an inspection about every six months just to check no fiddling was going on, but Dad would find a way round it.

In the spring Mother got some lodgers who had been sent from the London area to work at F. H. Lloyds, a local steel foundry. Two of them were painters, their job was to paint the factory in brown and green patches for camouflage but they only stayed a couple of months. Jack Atkins was an engineer and he stayed on. His father joined him for a while and later in the year when London started to get bombed, he brought his wife and daughter up to stay with us and they became great friends with my parents. We also had an evacuee, a young girl but she didn't last very long as my sister Mary made it plain there was only room for one girl in our house, so the evacuee had to go.

Mother now decided to take the 'Dig For Victory' campaign to heart and the first move was to divide the garden in half, which resulted in a trip one Sunday morning to Coles at Bilston with the horse and cart. This was a good outing for us kids and even better when we got there, as they had a brown bear in a cage in the middle of the yard. Mother bought enough old roof sheets to divide the garden and some second-hand wire netting to go along the top to keep the fowl out, and home we went.

Digging the garden was the next problem as it was a fairly big area so anyone who could do a few rows was roped in, Billy Stone a lad from the bottom of Gower Street did most of it, bribed with a few eggs and a couple of bottles of beer. Vegetables were planted in the top of the garden and potatoes along the bottom and we were never short of advice as there were always gardeners fetching barrow loads of muck from the farm for their allotments and they soon told us how to do it, they were all experts! Dad knocked up a cold frame for growing tomatoes and Mother would pollinate them with a lump of cotton wool on a stick. While she was doing it Dad lent on the fence making buzzing noises until Mother threw a watering can at him.

Our parents got very friendly with a couple of the soldiers stationed on the field, I think one of them, Ernie, they had known from their young days. Although Ernie now lived in Birmingham he had some relations in Wellington Street. He was a little chap with short legs and Dad used to say he had Ducks Disease, his arse was too near the ground. Ernie could play the piano so there were occasions when a spot of entertaining would go on in our posh room; beer would be fetched from the off licence in Dora Street and singing and piano playing would go on into the night. We kids could not sleep and we were all ears: as the night wore on some of the songs, like 'old cocky bendy' were sung which we were not supposed to be hearing.

We spent a lot of our time down at the pool at the bottom of the field fishing for tiddlers and paddling when the weather was nice, and although it was a bit muddy it didn't bother us much. It was down by the pool against the railway fence one morning, that Bill found a little furry animal which he picked up and cuddled. When we got back home and Dad saw what Bill had got (it was a rat) he knocked it out of Bill's arms and stamped on it; Bill was very upset.

Another place we spent a lot of our time was in the old sandpit where we built dens, dug tunnels, and even fortified it, making pretend guns out of bits of pipe.

The wenches spent a lot of their time organising little concerts in the A.R.P. hut where they would charge a penny to watch them perform with all proceeds going to the stirrup pump fund.

We had to help Mother a bit as Dad was now on his own since even old Harry Bagnal had been found a job sweeping-up in a factory.

In the late spring our parents had their ears glued to the news on the radio; the army was making a tactical withdrawal from Europe, well that was what they told us kids, it was a disaster really. As we understood it France had built the Siegfried Line to stop any invasions after the last war. Not having the benefit of an English Public School education and being foreigners as well, the Germans cheated, and went around it.

The Sunday morning conference in the yard discussed it; if they had been there it wouldn't have happened and they were not best pleased when Mother asked them if they were going to learn German. All the talk now was of us being invaded.

Churchill was now Prime Minister having succeeded Chamberlain in the summer of 1940. He was on the radio making stirring speeches, 'we will fight on the land, we will fight on the beaches', the 'we' being the royal we of course, as none of his tribe would be there with a gun in their hand.

The L.D.V. (local defence volunteers) was set up consisting mostly of men too old for the army. They had no weapons or uniforms, just an armband with L.D.V. on it. The setting-up of this was the opportunity the frustrated little Napoleons who had served in the first war had been waiting for. They soon appointed themselves officers-in-command and our first encounter with them was in the summer.

Mother had got some tickets for a show in aid of a wartime charity at a theatre in Brum, Granny would take the three of us and so we caught the Midland Red bus from Walsall to Brum. All went well until we got over the Scott Arms cross road and up the hill by Hampstead Colliery where the bus was stopped by three men wearing L.D.V. arm bands. They were looking for German spies and wanted everyone off the bus to check us out. The leader stationed one of his men in front of the bus so it could not drive off and then tried to get on the bus. The conductor shoved him off, saying he was not coming on his bus and nobody was getting off. While all this was going on, the driver sat in his cab having a smoke. An argument between the leader, conductor and some of the passengers went on until the driver had finished his fag and announced if the man standing in front of his bus didn't move he would run him over. The leader and his assistant then ran round to tackle the driver, who had locked himself in his cab. He started the bus and drove off, pushing the man in front out of the way with the bus. I can't remember much of the concert – all the fun had been had on the bus.

It was a good summer and I learnt to swim. Mother got Changy Chalinor, the son of one of her friends from Dora Street, to take me to the baths but I only went a couple of times. Swimming in the canal on our way home from school was how I, and most of the boys in my class learned and once you could swim you were allowed to go with the school.

An old teacher named Mr Pattison was in charge of swimming, which always took place in the last lesson of the morning. Cozers were rolled up in our towels, placed under our right arm and we were formed into a file and marched off down Walsall to the baths. After our swim we were left to our own devices to get home, have lunch or dinner as we always called it and get back to school for two o'clock.

When old Patto thought you were good enough he would enter you for the swimming test. For this you needed to dive in at the deep-end of the baths and swim six lengths. If you passed the test (as most of us did) you would get a book of ten tickets for free entry to the baths. Darlaston baths was where we went a lot with our friends. It was new, only built in the late 1930s and very modern. When the weather was nice we would swim in the pool at the bottom of the field and our Bill learnt to swim in there, a bit muddy but we enjoyed it.

A trip to the cinema to see *The Wizard Of Oz* was organised by Mother. One of her friends' sisters would take us three kids and her niece Doreen to the Savoy in Walsall to see it on Saturday afternoon. Mother gave her our bus fare and the sixpence each admission. When we got there, it was eight pence to go in so the woman paid for Doreen and herself, gave us our sixpences back and left us standing there. Mary and Bill stated to cry so I decided to do something about it. We caught a bus to Caldmore Green for the Forum cinema. I had heard about it at school and knew they had Saturday shows for kids; a main film, some cartoons and a weekly serial, usually a cowboy. Admission was three pence at the front and five pence at the back so we went in the three pence seats and had a great afternoon. I expected to get my ears boxed when we got home and Mother found out what I did, but I got ten out of ten for initiative although Mother still had the nine pence change back off us.

After this, Bill and I with our friends would go regularly. It was bedlam in there on a Saturday afternoon, with us kids cheering the heroes and booing the villains; if there had been a Cowboys and Indians film on, we would shoot our way home all down Watery Lane and through the Pleck.

In the summer Dad started to make preparations for his cows. Two of them named Mary and Rochford would calf later in the year; these two had been brought back from Barwells and put in the field while Dad made a cowshed. This was in the large barn opposite the house and next to Bonnie's stable. It had always been the farrowing pens for the sows but would now be our cowshed.

Dad had to work in the summer as there was no lighting in the out buildings, only candles and hurricane lamps, and as the days got shorter he would have little time to do much after feeding the pigs and the other things that needed to be done around the farm. A single-storey building on the side of the house would be the dairy. This had a large oven built in the back showing it had been a bakery at some time in the past. This backed on to the fireplace under a large inglenook that had benches round it in the room we used as the kitchen.

Equipment for the dairy like churns, cans and a milk cooler were acquired, a bit at a time, as the money became available, through Dad's brother Albert.

As the summer went on we kids played to our hearts content, little affected by the war. We gathered from our parents and school that things were not going very well and they were very concerned but to us kids it was a big game as we defended the sand-pit, swam, and helped Mother in the garden; scrumping the peas and turnips or 'Chonuks' we always called them.

Things became more serious when London was bombed for the first time and I think that was the start of what would be known as the 'Battle of Britain'. London would suffer regular attacks after this.

The only bit of the war we saw was on Saturday afternoons, when a yellow trainer plane from Aldridge Aerodrome would fly round doing aerobatics, I think this was just a propaganda stunt to make us think something was being done to win the war. The sirens would go off occasionally to warn of an air raid, but our first bombs near Walsall were in late June when some were dropped at Daw End and Great Barr. In late August the Public Works Depot in Bloxwich Road was bombed.

One Sunday afternoon in August, we had gone down the field with Mother to look at the cows due to calf. We could hear planes in the air and all of a sudden there was a burst of machine-gun fire. We all lay flat on the ground, as advised by the latest civil defence pamphlet, until all went quiet then ran home. We kids thought it a great adventure; we were part of the war now.

Mother and Granny Mac where now busy harvesting fruit and vegetables from the garden; tomatoes and runner beans were bottled, eggs put down in buckets of isinglass, apples wrapped in paper and placed on the floor in a spare bedroom, elderberry wine started. Billy Stone came and dug the potatoes up for them; these were dried and stored in the barn. The cupboard in the posh room was raided for sugar to make goosegog jam, with gooseberries harvested from a row of old bushes that grew at the back of the garden. Pears were sold to anyone who would buy them for a few pence, but at this time of the year we had plenty of fruit in the shops so the only shortages were imported fruit such as oranges and bananas.

When we started back to school after the summer holidays 1940, my brother and sister would join me in the junior school. I would be in my second year now, still struggling to read and write and sat on a desk along the front of the class, with all the other duff scholars in the 'wastrels club'. The only recollection I have of the teacher was that she was old; I can't remember her name at all. Music was now added to our lessons and would be held in the hall where the piano was. We didn't have any musical instruments to play, it was all singing, English folk songs being the order of the day like Barbara Allen, Early One Morning and Sweet Polly Oliver. Me being tone deaf didn't go down too well, so along with a couple more of the class who sang out of tune (all boys of course) we were found other employment, namely collecting old paper and cardboard from the shops in the Pleck for salvage to help the war effort.

The air raid sirens would now go off occasionally and there were a few incidents. We started to sleep in our air-raid shelter in the cellar. It was in November 1940 when Coventry got heavily bombed.

Most of our aircraft engine manufacturers were based in Coventry and the medieval town centre was devastated and the Cathedral burnt down. We would now get regular raids on Brum as there were several aircraft factories in the Castle Bromwich and Bromford area. We could watch the start before the actual bombing took place as the planes would come and drop flares to mark out the targets. However, bombing being mainly guess-work at that time meant that the bombs got scattered around Brum and the district a bit. Barwels on the Beacon had one of their barns hit on one raid. Most of the bombing took place at night, but some raids were carried out in daylight.

All the junior school were in the school playground one afternoon when we heard an aeroplane and the teachers came and rushed us into the air raid shelter. A German bomber flying very low had dropped two bombs on the gas-works, one had exploded puncturing one of the gasometers and the other one had failed to go off. The plane had then crashed in a field at Stone Cross. The reason it was flying so low was that there had been a raid on Sheffield and this plane had been hit and damaged by anti-aircraft guns. While we were in the shelter I would suffer one of my life's great disappointments. A tin of sweets was passed along the rows and as it went past the row in front of me I saw a spearmint tablet in the tin that was going to be mine! But when the tin of sweets got to me, some swine had pinched it.

The best bit was if there had been a raid at night because we didn't have to start school until ten o'clock the next morning.

We lads also found a new hobby, collecting shrapnel from the spent anti-aircraft shells; we would show off our collections at school and swap bits among ourselves.

Two of Dad's cows had calved in October, and another two would calve before Christmas; he liked the cows to calf in winter as the price of milk was higher due to the government subsidy. The first milk they gave after calving was known as beestings that was thick and dark and contained the antibodies the calf would need. They would be fed on it for their first couple of meals but there was always plenty left over and Mother would warm it up and give it us kids; it would separate when warm, 'the curds and whey' of Little Miss Muffet fame according to Mother.

Dad now had to keep a register of how much milk each cow gave so a man from the Ministry of Agriculture would visit us about every two months to check it against the receipts from Claridges as this would be what they paid his subsidy on. The milk was sold to Claridges who had a little dairy in Palfrey They would collect it after the milking morning and evening; some they would bottle, but most of their milk was sold from the can. They were a two-man company, dad Claridge delivering round Palfrey with his pushcart and the son going further afield in a van. We missed the man who had delivered our milk before we had cows, Totty Timmins; he delivered milk on a little push cart and was a walking comedy show with his jokes and tricks.

As we got into December Mother would go and visit some of her old customers who still owed her money. They all had jobs now but the cash was still very hard to prise out of them; she was probably hoping they would get the Christmas spirit and pay up but some did, some didn't. Dad reckoned they were only adopting Mother's own philosophy, as one of her favourite sayings was 'Fear God, honour the King, part with your money, the very last thing.'

One Saturday morning just before Christmas, we kids were lined up to check that we had washed behind our ears combed our hair and got clean shirts on. Granny Mac was taking us on a shopping trip to Brum-e-jum. We had been saving our pocket money for such an event so I had seven and a tanner to spend – I was rich! We caught the Midland Red bus from Walsall to New Street where the workmen were still cleaning up the debris from a previous bombing, so we were sent round into Corporation Street.

Granny took us into Lewis's Department Store and my abiding memory of it is the children's hairdressing department. They had little wooden horses for the kids to sit on while they had their hair cut, mind you it would be a lot more money than the tanner we paid old 'Cold Fingers' our local barber for haircuts. It was our first insight into how the other half lived. Our excitement became intense when we had our first ride in a lift, to us kids it was like a magic carpet. Granny splashed out and we had our lunch in Lewis's café, it was much better than the bag of jam sandwiches she usually fed us with when we went on an outing. We paid a visit to Santa's grotto and told him what we wanted for Christmas. He seemed a miserable old buffer to me and we didn't get a present off him, you had to pay an extra half-crown for that. Most of our money got spent, five bob of mine on a kit to build a model aeroplane, a Boulton and Paul Defiant but it never got made; the bloody thing defied my attempts to do it. Our day out was all we could talk about for the next week.

Chapter Four

As we moved towards Christmas 1940, all the school made plans for the usual few days' entertainment that would be put on before we broke up (teacher's pets and creepers please stand-up). Each class would do something such as a little play or singing but Bill and I didn't get picked to join the players; like me, Bill was in the 'thick as two short planks' brigade. Mary was in some little play I seem to remember but then she was always the scholar in the family. We all had a good time sitting on the floor in the school hall watching the plays and things and we finished off with a few carols. Then the teacher took us back to our classroom to collect the Christmas cards we had made for our parents and have a little party, well a paper cup of orange juice and a mince pie, before we broke up for the Christmas holiday.

A pig was chosen for the Christmas feast and Bill and I were roped in to help (hold the hurricane lamp) as this was to be done after milking and in the dark when the farm gates were locked. A large tin bath was placed under the boiler shed where Dad cooked the pig-food, filled with water and heated to near boiling. The pig was bought out, hit on the head with a hammer to stun it and then had its throat cut. We had to give Dad some help to wrestle the dead pig into the tin bath. The animal was scraped of all hair, then a slit cut in each hind leg and hauled up on a double swivel hook by pulley blocks and cut down the belly. Liver, chitterlings and anything edible was put into clean buckets, the rest would be buried in the muck heap. The pig was then split into two halves and taken over the yard and hung in the corner of the dairy for the pork to rest and set. Dad had strung a sheet across the corner of the dairy to hide it saying, 'what the eye don't see the heart don't grieve for.' The following evening the pig was cut up on the large wooden table in the kitchen, the head removed and the lard leafs taken out. The head would be made into chawl and the lard leafs rendered down for cooking fat and stored in earthenware jars. We saved half a leg for our Christmas dinner and Dad kept a leg and half a side to put down for bacon. The rest was cut into joints to be distributed round Dad's family and where it would do the most good on the 'you scratch my back and I'll scratch your back' basis. We now had to make room on the sill in the air-raid shelter (the cellar) for Dad to put the leg and half side down for bacon. He worked a little saltpetre down the ham bone, and then rubbed it all with salt, it was then put in the corner and covered in more salt. It would be a couple of months before it was ready to eat.

Christmas came but there would be no party in our posh room this year and no church bells would be rung for Christmas or the New-year since church bells ringing were going to be the signal we were being invaded. Granny Mac didn't need the bells to tell her when the 'God-shop' was open; she would be there, dragging Mary along with her.

The bombing raids had almost stopped so Jack Atkins and his family went home for a few days over the holiday. We all had a merry time chewing the pork crackling and bodging a rug but I can't remember what Santa bought me that year although he must have come with something. If he hadn't I would have remembered all right.

During the school holidays I gave Bill a haircut with some clippers Mother had hidden in the cupboard. She had got them by saving the tokens from cornflake packets. While she was out one afternoon, I got the clippers and cut a ridge right over the top of Bill's head with them. When it was my turn for Bill to cut my hair I wouldn't let him do it, he wasn't going to cut a ridge over my head. When Mother came home and saw what I had done to Bill I got a right thumping off her.

Dad let in the New Year 1941, or so we were told since we were asleep. We kids had been given a small tot of Granny's elderberry wine before going to bed but we didn't get a lot, just enough to wet our tongues and ensure we didn't get drunk and start fighting. Usually we only got a drop before bedtime if we had a nasty cold. There would be no party in the posh room this year; they had died out due I think to an argument about who was going to pay for the beer.

We started back to school and Mother found a beret for Bill to wear to cover his haircut. He was the second kid in the school to wear a hat in class; Harold Fellows who was in my class always wore a cap in the classroom. Bill didn't seem to mind his haircut; in fact he was rather proud of it like a Mohican haircut in reverse.

School was starting at nine o'clock most mornings now and our last daytime air raid warning had been well before Christmas. In January I was coming down Slater's Lane, on my way home for lunch when the sirens went off. The people in the last house in Kingsley Street were going into their shelter, as this was at the side of the Lane so they lifted me over the wall and took me in the shelter with them. I didn't mind as they handed round a tin of sweets when we were in the shelter, lucky old me. The warning only lasted for about half an hour then the all clear went and I ran home. I think this may have been the last daytime warning we had.

In January the pool was frozen over thick enough for us kids to play on and we had a great time. We would rush home from school to get an hour on the ice before tea. One of our games was ice hockey without skates or sticks, though some of us found old walking sticks to use. Some of the older kids with well off parents had proper ice skates. There were always plenty of kids to make the teams up; it attracted them for miles around. I found a pair of old ice-skates in the large cupboard in our living room that were made of wood with metal blades and had leather straps to fix them to your shoes. They belonged to Mother but she said I could use them if I black-leaded the fire grate for her. I never got to try them out as the thaw set in before I could use them so they would have to wait until next year. The pool was not very deep it only came up to our chest when we swam in it. I never remember anyone falling through the ice, but I suppose someone must have at some time. Dad always reckoned it couldn't be very deep as the water only came half way up the ducks' backs when they were in it.

It was about this time that we were taken by Mother and Granny one Sunday afternoon to the Arbo to see a German Messerschmitt fighter plane on show there (a 'Mrs Smith' Dad called it). It had been shot down while on a raid. It may have been there for War Weapons Week and it was only on show for a week so lots of people were there. I seem to remember that you had to buy a National Savings stamp to get in. I think Wolverhampton was the next town it went to when it left Walsall.

The piano was now to be the focus of attention at home; we were all going to learn to play it, so Mother said. A strip of paper was stuck above the keyboard and the notes marked off; doe, ray me, so, fa, la, tee, doe 'what makes me fart I do not know' was what we sang to it. Mother enrolled us at Miss Baggot's in Hilary Street opposite the school. This was a bad mistake, as all our school friends could see us going in there for our lessons after school. Things got even worse when Granny rigged us out with little leatherette cases to carry our music in. Bill and I got some ribbing about it from the rest of the kids in our classes. Bill and I hated going but Mary took to it like a duck to water and we were forced to persevere with it. I think one of the main reasons we hated it so much was that Miss Baggot was a vicious old cow, if you played a wrong note you got a warning the first time but the second time you got a sharp rap on the knuckles with her little cane – it hurt! We had to practise at home as well, always supervised by Granny but as she couldn't play the piano it was the 'blind leading the blind'. Bill and I used to lay awake at night trying to think up ways to get out of the piano lessons, as none of it worked we had to go. I got as far as being able to play a little tune, the words to it still echo in my mind:

'Daises, daises red and white aren't they just a pretty sight, growing wild amongst the grass, how I love them as I pass'.

I can't remember how far Bill got before we managed to escape but it happened during the summer holidays. I think the problem of rounding Bill and me up and getting us scrubbed-up ready to go was a bit too much for Mother or Granny, plus the fact that Dad was getting fed up of paying for the lessons. Mary carried on with the lessons for a while but she gave up later.

Granny Mac now went into the general hospital to have her gallstones out. She had been saving up for years to get them done and now with an endowment policy pay out from the Pearl Insurance she had the means. While she was in the hospital and not able to visit the church one of the soldiers on our field, a strong Catholic, had taken Mary to a service at the Mount – a Catholic church in Caldmore – and she had gone there not once but twice. On Mary's second visit, she had come home with a string of beads to count and say a prayer. When Granny came out of the hospital proudly displaying her gallstones in a little glass jar she was not a happy bunny; as far as Granny was concerned Mary had been consorting with the enemy, however singing their hymns louder and a extra tanner on the plate when they got back to St John's church squared it all up.

Most of our Saturdays were taken up in collecting pig food as Dad was now keeping over one hundred pigs. The waste he got from the hospital and the bakery was not enough to feed them and pig meal was strictly rationed, so we would go collecting peelings. The government had put large adverts in the newspapers and posters were put up urging people to save their kitchen waste for animal food and the town council had placed bins by some of the lampposts for the collection. They boiled it and you could buy it back from the council to feed your pigs but Dad didn't see the point of paying for it if you could get it free. Mother had gone round a lot of the houses asking people if they would save their peelings for us and most of them agreed as they were able to get a chicken for their Christmas dinner off us.

We collected from the streets by the farm and round the Pleck. Gower Street was always a tussle as Ernie Wood at the top of the street kept a few pigs and it was a race to see who got there first. We never fell out over it and it was all good fun. Dickinson Drive was one of our best collecting areas. It was a fairly large estate and most of the houses saved their kitchen waste for us. Dad had a truck made for us by Henry Boys to collect from this estate. Henry Boys were an engineering firm in Oxford Street and had been our neighbours at New Mills and were friends of the family. The truck itself was a nice easy running thing about four feet long with blow-up tyres. It had fairly high sides so you could get a lot of stuff in it and it was alright to pull when it was empty but a bit of a struggle when full of wet peelings. But, as we usually roped in a few of our friends to help, we managed it. Sometimes we would go with the horse and cart but we used this more as the nights got lighter and we could do a bit of collecting after school. Bill and I liked collecting the peelings after school as this left Saturday afternoons for us to get to the Forum cinema.

As we got towards spring Mother was on 'The Dig For Victory' campaign again due to its success last year, although some of the bottled vegetables had been a disaster. No one liked the bottled tomatoes at all. Mother had to fry them before we would eat them;

the beans were a bit rough as well. Getting the garden dug over was a problem but Granny Mac would do a couple of rows and we kids did a bit and slowly most of it got dug and planted. We got plenty of advice but very little help from the local allotment holders when they fetched their barrows of muck on a Sunday morning. The potato-growing patch was not dug this year; there was no point since there were always spuds to be had in the shops. Mother was unhappy as she saw it wasn't helping the war effort.

Dad was mooching in one of the lofts one morning, they were full of things that had been left by the previous owners, when he found what turned out to be a little butter churn and this was to be very useful as our butter ration was only 4oz a week. The churn was a glass jar that would hold about half a gallon and had a metal screw on top with a turning handle and gears. Two wooden paddles went down into the jar and these whizzed round when you turned the handle. Granny soon got it all cleaned up and working and made us a bit of butter. The only trouble was that you had to turn the handle forever to make a dab of butter, however every little helped.

The meat was rationed by price so you were allowed to buy so much and it was not a lot. People kept fowl and rabbits to kill for food, fed on tea leaves mixed with bran and waste greens plus collecting dandelion leaves in the spring; boiled peelings for the fowl was their menu. There were still some wild rabbits on sale. During the winter the King Brothers who had a fruit and vegetable shop in Palfrey would come round on Saturdays with a handcart piled up with rabbits at nine pence each. They would skin it for you but a lot of people liked to skin their own as Tappers' scrap yard paid three pence for a rabbit skin. You could also get domestic bunnies for your dinner from the stables of Massey's bakery. Jim Shilitoe the ostler had a loose box at the bottom of the stables with them all running wild in it so you could pick your own and Jim would give it the 'Dudley Poke' and skin it for you. The skins of domestic rabbits were always sought after to be made into hats and gloves. Some of the local tanneries would tan them for you for the cost of a packet of fags.

Our turn came when we had veal for dinner. One of the cows had a bull calf and Dad had recorded it born dead. After a couple of days he butchered it. Granddad Power got the skin through the tannery and had it made up into two weekend holdalls. Although Granddad had been retired a few years he still had a lot of influence in the leather industry around Walsall. Mother had one of the holdalls and everybody wanted one, they were black and white. I think Albert's wife (Dad's brother) had the other one although neither of them had any use for it.

The news on the radio seemed to cause a lot of concern to our parents since the war was going from bad to worse. They would be there for the evening news whatever they were doing. Churchill's speeches were another must for them and he was becoming a bit of a hero to some but we kids weren't allowed to hear what Granddad Power thought of him. Churchill certainly was no hero in old Georges book!

What had started as the L.D.V. had now metamorphosed into the Home Guard, and we would all be entertained by their Sunday morning manoeuvres in the park and on the fields. Dad's hayricks came under attack most Sundays; they were also used for bayonet practice on occasions. Enemy machine-gun nests were cleared out of our barn; it was full-scale war until the pubs opened at twelve o'clock. Some Sundays Dad would borrow one of the men from Fred Tow the officer in charge, to hold the young hog pigs while Dad cut them.

As we got to the month of March, Mother decided she was going to start selling milk, a brave idea as there were a lot of milk deliverers in our area. There was the Co-Op, the Midland Counties, Bescot Grade A, Totty Timmins and the Bromley Bros from the top of Dora Street, who sold milk in the mornings and delivered coal in the afternoons.

Before she could start, a can and measures had to be bought since brother Albert couldn't supply them as they had to be officially stamped by the weights and measures people. The can and measures were brought from Burgesses the agricultural merchants in the cattle market at Wolverhampton. It was a two-gallon can with three measures hung inside, a one-pint, half-a-pint, and a gill. A pint of milk cost four pence halfpenny but if you were pregnant or had a baby it was two pence halfpenny. You wouldn't think anyone would buy a gill of milk, but they did. Milk was rationed at three pints per person per week but in practice it didn't work. You just registered with a milkman and he would be allowed enough milk to cover the customers registered with him. This would be twelve pints a week for a family of four and they probably only used a pint a day. People who drank a lot of milk got round it by registering with two milkmen. Since we were producing milk and selling it, the odd gallon here and there didn't matter.

Mother got herself a couple of dozen customers mainly around the Pleck by offering a morning and evening delivery (the milk being fresh didn't keep very well specially in the summer). This encouraged the big spenders to have half a pint morning and again in the evening. She would go round delivering on her bike in the morning with the can on the handlebars and in the evenings she would sometimes walk and take one of us kids with her to help carry the can as it was fairly heavy even when empty.

It was on an evening delivery later in the year that sticks in my memory. We had taken a short cut across the park, (closed but we used to get through the holes in the fence) to Mrs Mansells in Bescot Road, a good customer as she had a large family. After her we had a couple of deliveries in Dickenson Drive and then to our next customer Shutt's fish and chip shop on the corner of Narrow Lane. By now it was pitch dark. Mother delivered Mrs Shutt's milk and set off up the lane while I stayed for Mrs Shutt to give me a few chips in a bit of newspaper before following after her. I could see the outline of my mother at the top of the lane just before The Three Horseshoes pub, when a man stepped out from behind Southalls fence and stopped her. I could see they were having words but I was too far away to hear what they were saying. All of a sudden Mother took a step backwards, swung her milk can round and hit the man on the side of his head knocking him back against the fence. When I reached her the man was lying flat out on the ground. Mother said, 'just leave him,' and we went to our next customer Mrs Shaw in Gower Street. When we got back home Dad said it should be reported to the police, but no one near us had a phone and it would mean going to the cop shop in Walsall, so nobody bothered. We never did find out what the man had said to Mother.

Chapter Five

Air raids had got less frequent but we still had them. Our nearest was when some bombs were dropped across the railway at James bridge, one falling in the garden of the Railway Tavern pub. This one failed to explode so the bomb squad came and cordoned the pub off and it took them about a fortnight to remove the bombshell. It was only after the publican got back into his pub they found out why it had taken them so long to clear it up. The bomb squad had drunk half the beer in the cellar while they were doing it.

A few weeks later we had our first fatalities in Walsall due to bombing. Five firewatchers were killed at a factory in Hospital Street and the bomb left a crater twenty-five feet deep and forty-five feet wide and a lot of houses nearby were damaged. Although the newspapers never reported any bomb damage and would just say there had been a raid in the area, everyone seemed to know where the bombs had fallen and after the all clear was sounded crowds would turn up just to see the damage.

In June clothing got rationed and we were issued with coupons, sixty each if I remember right but I think growing kids like us got more. A black market soon got going and like everything else on ration, if you had the cash you could get most things.

We were now starting to get more food from America although we didn't see much of it until later in the year; tinned meat and cheese were the main things. The tinned meat put the word 'Spam' into the English language. The cheese was not cheese as we knew it; it was processed and in blocks about four inches square and a foot long ('transmogrified' Dad called it). The wooden boxes it came in were much sought after as they made smashing little mouse cages. Although we had food rationing there were always plenty of vegetables and with full employment people had the money to buy them and as Granddad Power was fond of pointing out, food had always been rationed for working people, by the price of it.

In the spring Dad borrowed a Friesian bull off Percy Haynes who farmed down the Delves. The bull seemed a tame old soul but Dad warned us to keep away from him. Dad was more concerned about Clarence who lived with his parents on the Darlaston Road. He was a simple chap who just roamed the area. He was harmless, but tales about him were legendary, like he had once been a professor and was so clever it had sent him 'doolally'. Another was that he had been a great mathematician and that had tipped Clarence over the edge, but I think the poor old soul had been born like it. Dad, however felt he had to warn Clarence's parents about the dangers of a bull being in the field. As it turned out, Billy (that's what everyone called the bull) was as soft as an old brush and he just followed the cows around, although he must have had some go in him because he got the cows in calf.

The haymaking was easy this year. As the soldiers were still on the top field there was no hay to cut. Dad got his hay off the railway playing fields at New Mills. The army wanted to camp some men on there and with all the young men called up the football pitches had not been used so there was a good crop of hay on it. Dad got someone to mow it for him and then the army brought it and spread it on our field to dry. With the help of the soldiers it was soon harvested into a rick.

The summer was always a great time for us, as well as helping our parents we had lots of things to do, fishing for one. In the late spring some of the tiddlers would turn blue with red breasts, these were probably the males and were always a prize catch. The best way to get them was to tie a small worm on some cotton and dangle it in the pool. The fish would try and swallow the worm in one go and when you pulled the cotton out of the water the fish would be hanging on the worm, sometimes there were two of them, one on each end. This way you caught lots of tiddlers with one worm.

Bill and one of our friends, Jimmy Gannon made a little pool out of a large stone trough in the pig field and we kept the fish in there, but they didn't live very long as the pigs kept messing it up.

There were some bigger fish in the pool; mainly roach and these attracted the fishermen. Uncle Busty Taylor used to come fishing sometimes.

The frog spawning was another fun time, as we knew all about how it worked. Most of the classrooms at school would have a bowl of spawn in the springtime for us kids to watch while the spawn turned into tadpoles (taddies we called them). You didn't have to feed them as they ate one another. The teacher would keep them until they started to grow legs then tip them in the brook at the Springfield's.

After the taddies had developed into little frogs, the bottom field would be alive with them. One of the tricks practised by the crueller kids was to stick a straw up the frog's jotter and blow it up.

There was always a lot of wildfowl about the pool as they nested in the reed beds along the railway bank. A pair of swans nested and would have cygnets every year. The eggs of the Water Hens, Coots, Dabchicks, and Ducks were often stolen – well, eggs were rationed and wildfowl eggs made good eating. In spite of all this the birds seemed to thrive, as there were large reed beds by The Bog in the park and also in the fields on the other side of the main railway line for them to nest in.

The reeds were to cause Bill a lot of grief in the summer. We would make whistles out of them by cutting them off just below a joint and again just before the next joint in the reed. By putting a slit in the side you could blow it and in the summer Pleck Park would ring with the sound of them. To cut the reeds and put the slit in them you needed a sharp tool and we had one of Dad's old razor blades for the job. Bill managed to cut his finger with it and the cut turned septic. The poison ran up his arm and he had a lump in his armpit like a duck egg. Bill was taken to Dr Davis by the Brown Lion pub who recommended a hot kaolin poultice to be put on twice a day. Mother soon got going on it, much to Mary's and my amusement, as Mother had taken the hot bit literally and poor old Bill was getting them slapped on, they didn't half make him howl. It cured the whistle-making for a while, but it didn't cure Bill, he ended up down at the General Hospital for a week.

In the late summer the soldiers moved off the field as the director of operations decided they would be better somewhere else, the main raids had always been on the north side of Brum and their searchlight would be better used down there. They left the two large huts that had been their billets behind. Dad was rubbing his hands thinking he was going to get them, but just as Dad was about to claim squatter's rights on the huts they came and took them away.

George Oliver who was married to Barbara, one of our cousins (although we always called her aunty) would come and park his lorry some evenings behind the barn where the soldiers had hidden their lorry. George was a driver in the R.A.F. and if he was passing through the area would come and park his lorry and spend the night at home since he only lived in Dickinson Drive. We kids did alright out of it as Aunty Barbara took us to the Pantomime in Brum when Christmas came. I can't remember what it was but Tessie O'Shae was the star. Aunty Barbara treated us to party in a café after the Pantomime – we had never had it so good!

The summer came and it must have been good because I only remember it being sunny. The war didn't much affect us kids; we let our parents worry about it. We were busy defending the sand pit in the field and messing around in the pool. Along with collecting pig food and helping Mother we had little time for much else. When the school holidays came it was like getting out of jail and we would be on the go from dawn till dusk with our friends. I think it was during this holiday we were taken on a trip to visit one of Granny Mac's brothers, Charlie, who lived at Talk-on-the-Hill, Stoke-on-Trent. We caught the train at Pleck Station to Wolverhampton where there were notices posted all over the booking office asking 'Is your journey really necessary?' Granny must have thought it was. From Hampton we got the train north to Stoke then the bus to Talk-on-the-Hill. All I can remember is the train ride and that Charlie lived opposite a coalmine, but we probably had a good time, anyway it was a day out.

This year was the first time Bill and I got what was to become known as 'tubbed in the tank'. This took place in a large metal water tank at the side of the boiler shed. Here Dad stored the water that had been used in the milk cooler to mix with the pig food. Every time Bill and I got too mucky Mother would get us by the scruff of the neck and just broddle us in it to wash the worst off us, much to the amusement of all. On this day we had been in a little field at the back of the main barn where Dad kept his sows after he had weaned the piglets off them. The sows loved it in there. It was a right mud wallow especially after rain and they would stay in there until about a week before they were due to farrow again. Bill and I had gone in bird nesting and once we had got muddied up one thing lead to another and by the time we came out we were in a bit of a state. I think it was Dad's idea to dip us in the water tank but Mother was soon taken with it and every time we got too mucky we would get dipped then taken over the house and stripped off. The old washing boiler was lit for hot water to bathe us, but as this took some time Bill and I would be freezing by the time the water was hot enough.

Granny Mac did her usual round of visiting her sisters taking Mary with her, why her sisters never visited her I don't know.

Bill and I did better when Mary was away as she always had to be queen bee, and being a wench she got away with murder. However, we had a gang of friends (they came in handy at times) who helped with the pig food collecting. When it was raining we would play in the barns or in the house and we never seemed to get bored. If we did, one of our tricks when in the house was looking through the window, humming a tune and flicking our lips as we hummed, or singing an annoying song like 'How much wood could a woodchuck chuck, if a woodchuck could chuck wood', until Mother gave us a bang on the ear for making too much noise.

In the summer the Atkins family went back home to Bexley Heath as Jack and his father had finished the job they had come up here to do. Mother got two more lodgers, a couple who claimed to be man and wife, but Mother thought it very doubtful. We kids liked them. They didn't have their meals with us like the Atkins did, I think they took one look at Granny's cooking and decided to eat in the works canteen. They had come here to do a job at Rubery Owens and only stayed a couple of months before having to go somewhere else. We never found out where they came from or where they went. They were the last lodgers we had at the farm and when they left we never had any more.

September 1941 came and time to start back at school; Bill and I had a new pair of short trousers each to go in. Mother had made them out of an old tweed suit Granddad Power had given her to cut up for rug bodging, but she must have thought it would make good trousers. They had obviously been made for us to grow into; you couldn't tell if they were long shorts or short long trousers, Bill and I looked like refugees from 'poverty knob'. We got some nice comments from the other kids when we got to school.

As the new term at school started I didn't go up to the third year, I was moved along with four other kids into the second year 'clever clogs class'. There were two girls and two boys, Benny Whitaker,

Bessie Gregory, June Wilkes and me. We hadn't been the worst duffers in our previous class so it seemed someone was out to save us. We sat at the back of the class and not in the wastrels' row at the front. Mrs Satterthwaite was our teacher and we all liked her except Bessie because she was left-handed. Mrs Satterthwaite insisted that Bessie wrote with her right hand – there was going to be no left-handers in her class, the poor wench had a right struggle. My turn came one morning when Benny Whitaker gave me a ball bearing he had taken out of a bicycle wheel. I sniffed it up my nose and it got stuck. My attempts to get it back down attracted the attention of the teacher who dragged me out in front of the class but a nose blowing session had no success. Mr Brockhurst, the headmaster was sent for and there was a discussion as to whether I should be sent to the hospital or the school's clinic. A final nose blowing would be tried before a decision was made. I was to hold my head slightly back and blow hard, it worked and I got the bearing down. What happened next made me wish the bearing had stayed up my nose; Mrs Satterthwaite grabbed me by the back of my shirt collar and laid into the back of my legs with her cane, she gave me a right whacking.

One afternoon in the autumn on my way from school, I scrumped an almond off a tree in Councillor Bonner's garden at the bottom of Mountford Drive. His daughter Pauline was in the same year at school as me, but in the high flyers class. When Mary found out I had pinched the almond, she told our mother who confiscated it, although it was still all green and of no use. The furore that followed made me realise that I had committed the crime of the century. I got a thumping and was sent to bed with no tea. At about six o'clock, I was fetched down stairs and scrubbed up, Mother was already done up like a prize terrier. She was going to take me back to 'face the music', as she put it. She marched me across the park to Councillor Bonner's house to confront my crime. It now became clear to me that this was not about me scrumping the almond but a creeping session round Councillor Bonner. She was out to do a bit of brown nosing. Old Bonner took it all in good part; boys will be boys etc. and told Mother his almonds had always been taken by the kids and it didn't bother him. The tree was only ornamental and grown for the blossom; the fruit was of no use and couldn't be eaten. The discussion that has gone on since the start of the human race followed – kids of today not being the perfect little angels of our parents' generation, which went on for some time. During the talking and much to Mother's annoyance, Mrs Bonner had given me a piece of cake and a glass of pop. By now I could see Mr Bonner was trying to get rid of us; he probably wanted his tea, but it took another ten minutes to prise Mother out. If the object of this little trip was to get the Bonner's milk custom, it failed miserably. Mother was not too happy so I got a belt round the ear on my way home.

Chapter Six

Bottling and preserving food for the winter had now started and things that had not been a success last year were going to be all right this year. We had blackcurrant jam as well as goosegog this year as Mother had swapped a few eggs for a basket of blackcurrants off one of the allotment holders who came for some muck. Rhubarb and apple jam was also tried; there was a large rhubarb patch in the part of the garden Mother had not fenced off. By now the sugar stock in our store was starting to look a bit thin so we had to have saccharin in our tea and the sugar was to be kept for more important things.

We sold pears on Sunday afternoons. We would stand by the park railing with some scales if the weather was good and sell them to the people visiting the park. We only got about two pence a pound for them but it was better than nothing. Sometimes we would go round the streets with the pears in a barrow and sell a few just to make enough money to buy a bottle of pop and get us into the pictures. Our apple tree was never a heavy cropper so we never sold any. They were good eating, either dessert or cooking, Emperor Alexander was the name, so the expert told us. A few were given away but most were wrapped in newspaper and stored in a bedroom.

Most of the news of the war now was about the battles in North Africa at a place called Tobruk. To us kids it seemed someone called Rommel was the cause of the trouble. We were also having a lot of our ships sunk by submarines and all in all we didn't seem to be doing very well. The news reels when we went to the pictures used to show we were doing all right, but I think they were just putting a brave face on it. We always seemed to be waiting for the next disaster and it came in early December, for the Americans this time, not us.

The Japanese had attacked their naval base in the Philippines and sank a lot of their ships, although the Japanese and Americans were not at war. President Roosevelt and the Americans now declared war on both Japan and Germany, to our relief.

A lot of things not on ration were starting to get very short and Mother was forced to smoke other brands of cigarettes on the occasions she couldn't get her beloved Capstan. Off she would go with a fag in her mouth and one behind each ear, the packet stuffed in the top of her jumper.

I was doing a lot better at school but English was still my downfall – the spelling mainly and I have never learned to spell even to this day. By the Christmas holiday I was the second best in the class, June Wilkes was top banana.

Being in the higher echelons of the class meant I would now be in line for one of the starring roles in the Christmas play, so come back all I said about creepers and teachers pets! Mrs Satterthwaite came up with a little play about a fairy shoemaker and some goblins. I was to be the fairy shoemaker, and June Wilkes would be my wife. Schoolwork was not to be interrupted, so our playtime would be given up for rehearsals. A cobbler's last was borrowed from somewhere together with a little wooden mallet, well I couldn't be trusted with a proper hammer could I? No costumes would be needed for the play and all I got was a pixie's hat made out of crêpe paper. I cannot remember much of the detail now, but one line has stuck in my memory over the years, 'I cannot shirk and leave my work I'd feel so blue with nothing to do.' We worked hard on the play in the week leading up to the holiday and got it almost word perfect; we would show them how plays should be done!

The last few days in the school hall before we broke up seemed to go on forever while we were waiting to put our play on, then disaster struck. There was a backlog of the entertainments so the programme would have to be shortened and our little play was struck off the list. To say we were disappointed was putting it mildly, our careers on stage and screen all gone up in smoke. We sobbed our little hearts out, well June did; I was relieved I didn't have to do it, probably stage fright in my case.

There was no pop and mince pies this year, all we got were the Christmas cards we had made for our parents in art lessons.

It would be two pigs for Christmas this year but Bill and I were not called on to help. Jeff Slater was home on leave from the army and being a butcher by trade would come and help Dad. The slaughtering would be a secret after dark lantern-lit affair, same as last year, with

Joey the dog on patrol. With Jeff's help it didn't take them very long to do it. Dad had killed the extra pig to give to the people who had saved all their kitchen waste for pig food over the year. It was cut up into small joints, wrapped up and put in a clean dustbin ready for us to take round when we collected the peelings. Dad gave us strict instructions on how to distribute it. We would get it out of the bin in the corner of the float and place it in the bottom of the bucket we collected the peelings in and take it to the back door of the house. When they opened the door to us we were to ask them if they wanted a piece of pork, it was a daft question to ask, Dad's idea. Did they want a piece of pork? Didn't they just, couldn't wait to get their hands on it could they. We would hand it over, swearing them to secrecy as to where it came from.

The other pig was distributed around family and friends and where it would do the most good. Having two pigs' heads this year meant there was plenty of chawl made. The lard leafs would be rendered down and kept for cooking and pastry making. Most of it was given away to Dad's family; old George was always at the front of the queue.

We all had a great Christmas, stuffing ourselves with food. The secret store cupboard was raided for goodies and with what we had from the garden we never had it so good. Santa came and brought a large wooden fort with some cannons on top for Bill and me, we didn't get any new lead soldiers with it, we had to use our old ones. Mary got a doll's pram, a blue one.

By the time we should have started back to school we had all got the mumps, so we had to stop at home till they cleared up.

Dad let in the New Year, 1942, again and we kids thought we may get a little extra of Granny's Elderberry wine, being ill with the mumps' but we thought wrong.

The big freeze started in January and we had freezing weather until March; everything was frozen up. Our parents were not very happy about as it made their jobs a lot harder. We kids took a different view – it was fun. The pool was our main playground during the freeze-up; it was the opportunity I had been waiting twelve months for. Mother's old skates were found again and I soon got them strapped to my boots and I was on the ice. It was not as easy as I thought it would be so I had a few tumbles to start – I was like a 'fairy on a gob of lard' but I soon learnt. The skates proved to be a bit a problem when I tried to use them to play in the ice hockey games. Being the only one on skates they said I was cheating, but I couldn't skate that good. It was them that did the cheating, putting their sticks through my legs and tripping me up, so I took the skates off to play.

The next war disaster came at Singapore in February. The Japanese army captured one of the outposts of the empire and our main naval base in the Far East. The military experts had made Singapore impregnable by invasion from the sea but the Japanese being wily Orientals cheated and came overland.

The war now became more real for us kids as one of our friends Kenny Harding had a brother Harold who was lost when his ship was sunk during the battle for Singapore.

We also had our own disaster when Dad was taken to the General hospital with appendicitis. It couldn't have happened at a worse time, right in the middle of the coldest winter for many years and my main memory of it is just how cold it was. The roads were all icy so we had to take old Bonnie the horse to Norman Rounds to have frost nails put in her shoes before we could fetch the hospital and bakery waste.

It was all hands to the pump trying to run the farm without Dad. Granny looked after the house and did most of the cooking and Mary would help her when she came home from school. Bill helped Mother with the cows and I fed the pigs. Each night I lit the boiler before I fed the pigs. My main problem was getting the food from the boiler shed to the sties. I found the best way was to put a dustbin on the sack truck, put the swill in it and wheel it across the yard and pour it into the troughs with a bucket. After feeding, the cooking tubs were filled and the boiler kept stoked until Mother went to bed. This ensured the pigswill was cooked and still warm for feeding the pigs the next morning.

Mother made me an overall out of an old bran sack. She cut a slot in the bottom to put my head through and a slot in the sides to put my arms through and I wore it like a long vest, down to my ankles. Bill and Mary thought it was hilarious and called me 'sack man', but it kept most of the muck off me.

Bill's task was feeding the cows and taking the milk over the yard and putting it through the cooler. He also did a bit of milking which helped Mother a lot.

We got some help on the weekend with lifting hay and bags of meal from Fred Tow who would detail a couple of his Home Guard to help us out. People were very good, working until six thirty at night but we had usually fed the pigs and done the milking by then although it was kind they offered to help.

Collecting the peelings went on mainly with the help of our friends on Saturday afternoons and Sundays, bribed with oatmeal biscuits cooked by Granny Mac.

Dad spent a week in the hospital and was kept in the house for a week to convalesce when he came home. Dad was chomping at the bit to get on the yard but Mother wouldn't let him out. He needed help with heavy things for a couple of weeks. Bill and I were still needed to muck in a bit after school; we had just about survived and we probably only lost a couple of half days each of school through it all. With the weather picking up in late March things soon got back to normal.

The four of us who had been in Mrs Satterthwaite's class were now back in the form we should have gone in last September. I can never remember the teacher's name, she was a young tall lady who wore glasses and she must have been good, as all the kids liked her. One of my abiding memories is of her reading to us on Friday afternoons; I remember especially the story of Robin Hood. It was while in her class that the headmaster of the school came and fetched me out of the class one morning just as we were about to start lessons. The dogs had followed Bill and me to school this morning and I thought they had gone back home when we got to the school playground, but they couldn't have done. Mr Brockhurst took me to Bill's class where our two dogs, Joey and Mick were racing round the classroom. The kids were shouting and jumping on the desks and some of the girls were screaming which made the dogs even more exited. Bill could only grab one dog at a time and no one was prepared to grab the other so they had fetched me to do it. Bill and I soon rounded them up and the teacher gave us a stern warning and the consequences if it ever happened again. Mr Brockhurst by now had done a vanishing trick; he didn't like the look of Joey. The teacher gave Bill and I an hour to take the dogs home and get back to school before playtime at ten thirty.

We were never allowed to play football in the school playground and tip-cat was also banned. We spent our time playing jacks, marbles and another favourite was leapfrog. There were also still a few fag cards from before the war to swap and play with.

Mother was still taking the 'Dig for Victory' campaign seriously so it was all go in the garden. Granny Mac was appointed head gardener this year, as Mother was too busy delivering milk. Anyone who could do a bit of digging was roped in to help; Billy Stone did a lot of it for the usual bribes. It would be the last time he helped as he was called up for the army later in the year.

With Granny being in charge of planting we had a few flowers this year and with all the advice from the muck fetchers and two years' experience we did well for vegetables again.

It was now decided that we should have some rabbits since everyone else had them, so we should. Bill and I knocked up hutches in a little room at the end of the barn along the field with the help of some of our friends. We made them out of some old boxes and pinched Dad's wire netting for the fronts; they were not very smart but they would hold rabbits. Mother swapped a couple of young fowl for a couple of rabbits and we became rabbit keepers. Mary was put in charge of feeding, with cow nuts, hay and our leftover cabbage stalks and vegetable tops. The rabbit keeping didn't last long as we always had meat and once the novelty of having them had worn off no one wanted to bother with them, so Mother sold them to one of her friends.

We kids were glad to see the back of them, as the room we had kept the rabbits in had been one of our favourite play areas. On the back wall was a row of pegs, where the men who turned out their horses in the field hung the harnesses. On the other side were the benches where we had put the rabbit hutches. A flight of steps ran down to a cellar that was the whole length of the barn. The steps to the loft had gone but it was no trouble for us to climb up the wall to it. To us kids it was magic, our gang hut.

Chapter Seven

As we got into spring 1943 our usual summer pastimes started again; fishing, defending the sand hole and climbing trees. There were six big elm trees around the little field we called the meadow and wood pigeons nested in a couple of them. One tree at the end of the field always had owls nesting in it. Our favourite tree for playing in was always the oak tree on the path that led from the farm to the bottom field. It had long spreading branches ideal for putting rope on for swings and a few of us fell out of it from time to time but I don't remember any of us seriously hurting ourselves.

It was up in this tree that I had my first cigarette. We had turned our pockets out as we were coming down Hilary Street on our way for home from school and found we had enough money to buy five fags. I can't remember who went in the Post Office in Dickinson Drive and bought the fags, but it was probably Tucker Salt or Skally Plant. Woodbines were the cigarette everyone smoked at the time, but we being a bit exotic bought Park Drive. We couldn't smoke them on our way home across the park, as we didn't have enough money to buy matches, so I had to go home and pinch a couple. It was decided that if we got up the tree no one would see us smoking although they would have to be deaf not to hear the coughing. I was soon hooked and spent the next fifty years happily puffing away.

The emphasis was now on getting the farmers to produce as much food as possible to help the war effort. We were still getting some food from abroad but a lot of our ships were being torpedoed at sea and by now the government were getting desperate. The Ministry of Agriculture sent a man to see Dad with the view of getting him to have more cows. Dad was already planning to do this and he had kept a couple of heifers, Mary and Rochford's first calves and they would be in milk by the autumn. To accommodate more cows we would need a new cow shed, it was already a bit of a squash to get six cows in the one we had.

Some men from the council who owned the farm arrived one morning in May to do the feasibility study; there were four of them, two in bowler hats obviously the directors of operations. After a good look round it was decided to turn a row of piggeries that ran down from the main barn to the muckheap into a cowshed. This was chosen because it already had a little room at the end and a passage along the back.

The builders came a couple of weeks later and made a start on it. The tiled roof was taken off and replaced with asbestos sheets with skylights in. A row of twelve stalls was made down the length of the shed and the passage along the rear was left so you could feed the cows while they were in the stalls. The room at the end was also kept to store the cattle food in.

Dad gradually got up to ten milking cows and he would chain the bull in the end stall during the winter and in the summer. Jacko, one of the yard cats, always had a litter of kittens in the manger. The workmen who did the cow shed were always good with us kids, making mouse cages and things and one even made Mary a school desk. Some of our friends got jars of building sand for their elder sisters to sand their legs with. Silk stockings were hard to get so they would dye their legs with sand and put a line down the back with an eyebrow pencil so it looked like a seam. It looked alright until they got caught in the rain.

It only took the builders about three weeks to complete the whole lot and they whitewashed it all out. Before they left Dad managed to win a couple of bags of cement off them as well – it had been a good deal for all.

The old cowshed was now turned back to farrowing pens for Dad's sows. He was fattening more pigs than he could breed now and having to buy in store pigs. He needed the extra pigs because a lot of people were now keeping them in their gardens and came to our farm to buy one or two. Dad made a few bob on each sale and they got their pigs for a reasonable price, so everyone was happy.

On Monday morning Dad would go buying at Lichfield Market. In the markets of Wolverhampton and Lichfield the pigs for sale would be in pens of anything from four to ten and if there was a couple of pig clubs bidding against each other, they never knew when to stop and would bid eye-watering prices.

The only thing I remember about the rules for keeping pigs for food is that you were not allowed to kill a pig less than five score, (100 lbs) in weight. I think we may have been allowed one pig a year per family and I don't recall an upper limit on size. Dad would plan our pig carefully, he always reckoned the more mature pig made better bacon and we had to turn it into ham and bacon, as we didn't have a freezer. A nice long-bodied gilt (a young female pig) of about twelve score (240 lbs) would be chosen from pigs ready for slaughter and later put in pig. After her litter had been weaned she would be fed well for about a month before being killed and put down for bacon.

With Dad agreeing to have more cows, he may have qualified to have some help because we had a girl from The Women's Land Army come to live with us. I think she lived in the Burntwood area, as I remember her going on the bus to visit her parents most Sundays. She was in her early twenties, a blonde girl called Maisy and a big hit with us kids although Mother wasn't too keen on her. She could milk cows but wasn't too keen on the pigs; she didn't mind feeding them but didn't like cleaning them out, however she was a big help.

The hay crop this year was off Elwell's sports ground at Woodgreen and Dad got Cyril Barwell to cut it for him. Maisy drove old Bonnie in the hay-rake and we kids did the tedding. It took nearly a week to get it all done and as it was a distance of about four miles from the farm so Dad made arrangements to build the hayrick on the edge of the sports field. The haymaking must have been done during the school holidays, as I can't remember having time off from school.

The decision to build the hayrick on the sports field turned out to be a disaster, as the local kids played in it and wrecked the whole lot. A couple of cart loads was salvaged, brought home and stored in the barn, before what was left got set on fire. This was the last year we harvested our own hay; in future Dad would buy ready baled.

We got a rude awakening in late July 1942; with an air raid very early one morning. Things had been quiet for some time so we had been sleeping in our beds so Mother had to get us all down the cellar when the sirens went off. It didn't last very long and we had our first bit of damage; two broken windows caused by shrapnel from the anti-aircraft guns. Dad had to board up the windows for a while as you couldn't just go to the builder's merchants and buy glass any more, you had to prove the need for it and get a permit from the Town Hall before you could buy it.

During this raid the Walsall Corporation bus garage was set on fire and some of the buses burnt out. These were replaced by some open-topped buses sent up from the London area, of course all us kids had to find an excuse for a ride on the top deck of one. 'Was our journey really necessary?' as the posters kept asking us, well of course it was, we had never been on an open-topped bus before!

A Church at Darlaston was also hit in the same raid and reduced to a pile of rubble. Granny Mac took us up to see it a few days later so we had joined the bomb damage tourists. The Church was just a pile of rubble; a land mine had been dropped on it so we were told.

We broke up from school for the summer holidays and Mother found out all our old clothes for us to wear (we had to keep the good stuff for our return to school in late August). Some of the older boys would go back to school later as they were given extra holiday to help with the harvesting.

Some of our friends had gone to the Walsall Schools Camp in the Hundred Acre Wood at Streetley for a week. I think they only took lads who had never been away before or if they had an elder brother going. Bill and I were never invited to go.

One of the highlights of our holiday was Mary being bitten by Parlow's dog. June Parlow was one of Mary's school friends. June's Mother had a milliner's shop on the Darlaston Road and Mary would sometimes go and play up there. All was well until Mary came home one day crying, Parlow's Bull terrier had bitten her on her behind and she had the teeth marks to prove it. Bill and I couldn't stop laughing and that only made Mary worse and really got her 'blartin'. The howling got even louder when Granny dabbed it with Iodine. The dog didn't suffer any ill affects, which surprised us all and Mary soon got over it.

We did a lot of fishing during the holiday using canes for our rods and we found that if we used the pliers Dad broke the little pigs' teeth with, you could make great little fish hooks out of pins. If we

55

were lucky the fishermen would give hooks to us, two I remember well are Finny Humphries and Jimmy Ash. It was Jimmy's idea to make a stage to fish from using an old cart on the field side of the pool.

There were two old flat four-wheeled carts that had been left by the previous tenants in what was left of the cart shed. Jim got Dad to let him have one and with some help pushed and pulled it down to the pool. The edge of the pool was very muddy and the wheels sank in so we couldn't get it in any further. Jim had been hoping to get it to the line of reeds that marked the stream, the blocking up of which had caused the pool.

All was not lost however; a man came round a couple of months later looking to buy old carts to refurbish. The man was interested in both the old carts as they had sound wheels and Dad soon did a deal with him and sold them.

September saw us back to school, which was hard to take after a month running wild, but we soon got used to it again. I was not in the front desks anymore so I must have 'pulled my socks up' or Mrs Satterthwaite had sorted us out during our time in her class.

During school playtime we were now into army cap badges since many of the lads had got them from their elder brothers who were in the forces. Some had come from James Bridge Copper works. If you knew someone who worked there you were all right for a few as they had bags of old badges to melt down. A lot were stolen from the factory as there was only a wire fence round the scrap-yard and you could put your hand through and grab them.

The best thing to have though was a dummy hand grenade (real grenades with no explosive in them). These were really a collector's item although a couple of the lads had them. The Home Guard used them when they practised their manoeuvres in the park and would sometimes lose one in the long grass. Finding one was like finding the pot of gold at the end of the rainbow. If you had one you had to be very secretive because if the teacher knew you had one they would confiscate it. We found one in the old hayrick once but Dad took it off us and gave it back to Fred Tow.

The annual jam making and preserving for the winter was now in full swing. With Maisy to help, things were going well and she was a big help to Granny Mac. Mother was a bit hard on Maisy, saying 'she will never die of hard work' and 'if she spent as much time looking after cows has she does chasing the boys, we would get more milk!'

We had a good pear crop so a few bob was made by us kids selling to people visiting the park on Sunday afternoons.

In November the church bell rang for the first time in three years in celebration of a victory in North Africa. Our parents had been following the battles as Aunty Sarah's eldest son Bill was out there as an army cook. Dad always said he was chasing the German army with a frying pan. Suddenly the world seemed a brighter place, as it was the first time anything good had happened since the war started.

The class contribution for the school Christmas concert would be a singing quartet of all wenches. I only remember one of them, Heather Steery who was one of the evacuees from London. The teacher kept them in the classroom at playtime to rehearse their songs, popular ones of the times like 'Silver Wings in the Moonlight'. At the concert, before we broke up for our Christmas holidays, they were the hit of the show.

Dad killed a couple of pigs again for Christmas. This was for the pig food savers since after last year's pork present they would expect it. We kids had to do the 'secret service' deliveries again. The family all got a joint with some liver and a bit of chawl, so everyone was happy. Maisy went home for Christmas Day and Boxing Day so this would mean extra work for Mom and Dad. The cows still had to be milked twice a day and although the pigs were fed one good meal to last them the day on Christmas morning they would be back to being fed twice a day on Boxing Day. We didn't get a lot from Santa this year, knitted socks and pullovers for Bill and me and Mary got a blackboard and easel to go with her desk. All had a great time.

Chapter Eight

The winter of 1943 was not as cold as the last one and didn't last as long, but it still knocked Dad about. He would sit in his armchair by the fire most nights coughing and wheezing. Mother's fag smoke and the coal fire didn't help his chest much either. Dad was always looking for a cure and would send us kids to Bernard Evans, the chemists to fetch him all the latest wonder cures advertised in the newspapers. Mother always reckoned he would end up poisoning himself one day.

It was fetching medicine for Dad one afternoon that got Bill a thumping. Bill had been sent to the chemists for some medicine and had come back with a tin of Andrews Liver Salts. That was not what he had been sent for so he had to take it back. Bill got the lid off the tin on the way back to the chemists and put some of the salts in his mouth. The salts all foamed up and Bill was going along telling everyone he was a horse foaming at the mouth, much to everyone's amusement. When Bill got to the chemists Bernard Evans could see the tin had been opened and wouldn't have it back, so Bill got a clout round the ears and sent to bed when he got back home.

Dad was under a Dr Thomson, who at this time had his surgery on the Wednesbury Road. After Dr Thomson had visited Dad, one of us kids would have to go to his surgery to collect whatever 'jollop' the Doctor's chemist had made up for him. It never cured Dad and he always had a bad chest. The house was cold and damp and although a good fire was kept burning in the big grate with two large kettles on the hobs, (our hot water system) it was like living in a barn and didn't help Dad's chest at all.

As we got into the spring 1943 Dad got a bit more help with the farm at the weekends. Ken Taylor one of Aunty Sarah's sons had now left school and started work in Walsall. Ken would now come and spend Saturday afternoon and Sunday with us. Being older than we kids (fourteen) he was allowed to be in charge of the horse and cart on our pig food collecting missions. Ken would go home to Shelfield on

Sunday night; there was only Gordon and him at home as his three elder brothers were all in the forces. With the help of Ken, Dad got the all the pigsties whitewashed and they found a quick way of doing it! A stirrup pump was borrowed from the A.R.P. and used to spray the whitewash onto the sty walls. This was much quicker than a brush. A good clean up of the pump before it was taken back and no one was the wiser.

With Ken and Maisy to help, Mother's 'Dig for Victory' gardening got a boost this year, she even got some potatoes planted. I can remember them well, 'Arran Banner' they were called and she got them from David Jones seed and corn merchants in Corporation Street.

Just as our garden was on the up and up, the allotment holders along the side of our top field were having trouble. One of Dad's cows was getting under the fence onto their plots and causing a lot of damage. She was Rochford's first calf and was called Heck; she would lie down on her side and wriggle under the bottom strand of barbed wire. She had become a right little escape artist but Dad had a plan to stop her tricks. A chain collar was made with a pole about two feet long attached to it and fitted round her neck. This didn't interfere with her grazing and normal activities but when she lay down to wriggle under the fence, the pole stuck up vertically and stopped her getting under it. Heck turned out to be a poor milk producer so Dad sold her later that year and bought another cow to replace her.

I was ten years old in March and I did alright for my birthday, I got a little brass steam engine for my present. We had many happy hours on wet afternoons with it going flat out on the kitchen table. It was probably the best birthday present I ever received.

A couple of days after my birthday Dad had to fetch the vet to his horse, old Bonnie, as she had gone very lame and he had to borrow Sid Perrin's horse for the day. Nelson was his name as he only had one eye. Sid only used Nelson a couple of afternoons a week to do a bit of hawking of fruit and vegetables. Bonnie never recovered although the vet tried several cures and the poor old soul had to be put down in the end. Several trips to the Lichfield market to buy a horse were made without much success as good horses were hard to find. The strict petrol rationing had meant horses were in great demand and fetching good prices.

Dad finally managed to buy a horse in Lichfield Market, a four-year-old cob named Bob. He was a heavier built horse than old Bonnie, so a new set of harness was bought from Pedley Bro's in Wolverhampton Street. Bob was a lovely bay-coloured horse with four white socks and a blaze on his head but being young and frisky was a bit too much for Dad to handle. He was not too bad in the traffic until he met a steam lorry and he didn't like them at all so another horse had to be looked for. Dad had a stroke of luck this time as Elise's Bakery in Caldmore was closing down and they were getting rid of their delivery horses. Dad bought an old mongrel of a horse named Harry off them; he was cheap and did the job for us. Harry's only claim to fame was biting Mother on the neck one day when she fed him and she had a right bruise on her neck and shoulder for weeks after. Bob was now turned out in the field and was later sent to a firm of horse breakers in Penkridge to be retrained.

Our parents now stated thinking about getting a little motor van instead of a horse, but with the war they had little chance of getting one. They put their names on the waiting list for a van at Reginald Tildesley's the Ford dealers in Lichfield Street, but it would be a long wait!

The war in North Africa was still going well; Montgomery was the hero of the hour according to the newspapers. He had saved Churchill's bacon, old Grandad George reckoned.

Most of North Africa had been retaken now and there was to be a thanksgiving ceremony in the Arboretum, a circus tent had been set up to hold it in. Granny and Mary went but was not impressed as it was for all denominations; they had been forced to consort with the enemy, was their view of it all.

There was no electric supply to the farm but the houses just outside in Gower Street had it so Dad had a plan to get it installed; he would offer the long cellar under the barn by the field as a rifle range for the Home Guard. They would need electric in the cellar and once we had a supply on the farm we were home and dry for getting the house connected. The Home Guard officers thought it a good idea and the local bigwigs came and did the feasibility study. However, the electricity board soon put the block on the plan – no new connections during hostilities, only repairs. So we would have to make do with gas and gas mantles were getting hard to find these days.

Our spring activities were now centred in the old sand pit in the field. There had been some attempts to fill it in once, but the top end of it was still a sand face. It was here that Bill and I along with some of our friends decided to dig a tunnel. We borrowed tools out of the farmyard to make a start on it after school and weekends when we were not collecting pig food. Being sand we thought it would be easy to dig, but it proved to be hard going but we stuck at it. After a couple of weeks we had probably got a tunnel about four feet in diameter and five feet deep, big enough for six of us to sit in when it was raining. No one thought it needed support and the inevitable happened, it fell in while Ronnie Hammond was digging in it. With the tunnel not being very deep Ronnie didn't get buried, although he got sand in his eyes and hair. The tunnel digging was abandoned for the time being.

A lot of American soldiers were now in Walsall town centre and they had taken over the Stafford's barracks in Lichfield. There were also a few stationed in some Nissan huts on the Mellish Road. Everyone was a little envious of them as their uniforms were better than our best suits and they always seemed to have plenty of money. They were very friendly and generous with the locals and a big hit with the young ladies. If we kids met one our standard phrase was 'got any gum, chum?' if we were lucky we might get some.

One of Ronnie Hammond's elder sisters married an American Army Officer who was stationed at Lichfield and that got the tongues wagging. Her husband was having her clothes sent from America since they didn't have rationing. As a result, Ronnie's sister was going around dressed up like a 'prize terrier' much to a lot of people's annoyance but good luck to her, we thought.

We had an American army officer from Lichfield come to our school and give us a talk about life in the U.S.A. We kids were fascinated and all ears as he told us about the food, clothes and all the good things of life. This was how it would be in Britain after the war, so we thought but we were to get a big disappointment.

Granddad Power came one day on the scrounge. As usual he was always alone as Granny Power never came. The only time we kids saw her was when we went with Dad to fetch the spent barley grain from Highgate Brewery. Dad would sometimes call in to see his mother on his way back home and would always leave her a few bob for a bet on the horses before he left. Dad's mother Elisabeth loved a little flutter on the 'Gee Gees'. Like everyone else she never won much and Mother reckoned Dad caught the gambling bug off his mother as he liked a little dabble on the horses but was more cautious as he always bet each-way. Granny's bet was three-penny doubles, two-penny trebles, and a penny roll-up all for a tanner bet. My main memory of paying her a visit is of a Sunday morning, Dad had sent us three kids to go and see her and had given us a few bob to take to her. Bill took his dog, a young Border Collie call Bob, along with us. On the wall at Granny's there was a large framed picture of old George proudly wearing his blue sash with his M.B.E. on it. When Bill's dog saw the picture he went berserk and we had to lock Bob outside the house until we went home. When we got home and told Mother what had happened she gave Bob a fuss, saying he was very perceptive and a good judge of character.

Chapter Nine

With Maisy and Ken now helping us collect the pig food we kids had more time to waste. We made a little gang hut out of the remains of the tunnel in the sand hole, using some old bits of corrugated sheet. It was half way between the farmyard and the pool, and we could have a crafty smoke in it without anybody seeing us. If we were in our usual little room at the end of the barn someone would see us. Most of our friends were in to having a crafty fag now, all except Bill and he never did smoke.

We broke up for the summer holidays in July as usual but with great expectations this year. Bill and I had been promised a week at Fradley with Granddad Power at his hut on the junction of the Trent and Mersey and Coventry Canals. Granny Mac along with Mary were planning to visit Granny's sister in Devon. On the Saturday morning Granny Mac took Bill and I on the bus to Lichfield where we met old George. Granddad had walked down from Fradley, a distance of about four miles and was planning to walk back with Bill and myself but Granny Mac gave Granddad George the money for a taxi so we went back in style.

Granddad's hut was at the side of a field with a little hawthorn hedge around it and a vegetable plot to one side. The water supply was an old hand pump in the field behind the hut. When we were sent to draw some water, we were strictly instructed by Granddad only to draw the water we needed and to do it gently. The pump was so old that if we broke it he would never be able to get the parts to repair it.

Around the junction of the canals were a few houses and a pub called The Swan; a Mr Woolly was both publican and farmer as it was also a farm. In the fields at the back of The Swan Uncle Busty and Aunty Sarah had their hut but they only came weekends.

Fradley was a favourite place of the Power family. Cousin Gordon stopped a few days with us at Granddad's hut and old George would send him over the wood some nights to set a gin trap to catch a rabbit. We never went with him, as Granddad wouldn't let us.

Old George bought the stale loaves from the Co-Op baker, as it was cheaper so the bread was rough. We still got it down us and Granddad's food was all right, if a bit plain. On a couple of days for lunch we had one of his famous Salute puddings (stale cake with custard on it). These puddings were a legend in the family.

Bill and I spent hours in the woods and running around the canals but we were more fascinated with the aerodrome at Fradley. There were Wellington bombers stationed there, and they made bombing raids on Europe at night. Most of the activity on the aerodrome was at night and early morning, but I can't recall the noise ever disturbing us as I think the woods may have deadened the noise of their engines.

When Granddad went down The Swan for a couple of pints after tea he would take us with him. Bill and I would get a bottle of pop and crisps each and told we were never to tell our Mother we had been standing about outside a pub. If Aunty Dora was staying with Mrs Keen (the lockkeeper's wife) for the weekend she would sometimes buy us a bottle of pop as well.

On Saturday nights there would a party in The Swan with Granddad, Uncle Busty, Aunty Sarah and friends. One image of it that always sticks in my mind is of old George curling his bottom lip up to suck the froth of his beer from his walrus moustache.

Both Bill and I had a great week with Granddad at Fradley and we would have liked to stay longer but Granddad was going home on Sunday so we came back with him. He gave us a rabbit Gordon had caught to bring home. We were met at the Walsall bus station by Granny Mac on Sunday evening and taken home.

While we had been at Fradley the war had taken a new turn. The allies had invaded Sicily and to most people it was said to be the beginning of the end. Anyway, we were back fighting on Europe mainly due to troops and supplies from the Americans. By the time we were back at school after our summer holiday, the allied armies had landed on Italy.

The summer holidays seemed to go by in no time and we were back at school early September. I was in Mr Pattison's class now for my last year in the Junior School. We knew old Patto as he was in charge of the swimming classes although it wasn't until years later we all found out the old bugger couldn't swim a stroke. He always carried a bent silver tanner in his pocket and would get it out to show the class at every opportunity. Old Patto was a veteran of the First World War and had shot the tanner while practising on the rifle range and he was very proud of it. Although I was never the class scholar I did all right while in his class and I even got picked to sit the eleven plus exam, I failed of course! The worst bit of being in his class was in the spring and summer. Patto was a gardener and grew his own tomatoes, so every month or so he would get me to bring him a bucket of cow muck to school. He would mix it with water to make liquid manure and feed his tomatoes with it. I used to dread him asking as it pulled my arms out carrying it across the park to school.

We had the autumn round of preserving food for the winter and although half of the stuff from last year had been thrown away Mother was always keen to do some more. She saw it as doing her bit to help the war effort. With Maisy to feed and Ken at the weekends we needed all we could save.

Dad now had eight milking cows and along with the pigs to feed, he didn't have much time. In the week he would milk and feed the pigs twice a day with all cleaning out and repairs done on Sunday when Ken was there to help him. The collecting of pig food became harder as the days got shorter since we only had the weekends to do it. We kids spent our Saturday afternoons collecting the peelings with Ken in charge of the horse and cart.

I didn't get picked for the class play at the school Christmas concert this year. My cobbler part in Mrs Satterthwaite's class seemed to be the highlight of my acting career. We all had a good time in the school hall before we broke-up; well, we were dodging lessons and that made us happy.

Although Dad was very busy he still killed a couple of pigs for Christmas so we kids were called on to do the secret pork distribution again. The family got their share and Maisy had a joint to take home to her mother.

When Santa came, it was with knitted presents again and we spent Christmas afternoon in the posh room with the gramophone going. What more could we want!

Chapter Ten

The New Year 1944 was let in with the usual ceremony, but we still only got enough wine to wet our tongues. It was parsnip wine this year; Granny Mac was keeping the elderberry for herself.

Dad was suffering with his chest again and the winter didn't help although we didn't have a bad one this year. Dad would sit in the alcove by the fire after he had finished the milking in a big wooden armchair coughing the night away. He was very proud of this chair and claimed it had once belonged to Sister Dora, although no one really believed him. The Matron of the hospital had given Dad the chair one day when he fetched the kitchen waste. I think that's probably where the Sister Dora story came from.

I was eleven in March but I didn't do as well as last year's Steam Engine for my birthday. I think my present was a pair of gloves. We got cake and jelly with our tea; the jelly was made in a glass rabbit mould. If we ever had a celebration of some kind we always got jelly or blancmange in that rabbit-shaped mould. It was another of Mother's little gems got by saving tokens off breakfast cereal packets; this was how she seemed to acquire most of her little treasures. Mother always put a bit of a party on for our birthdays although Bill and Mary being twins only got one party and this never went down well with Mary. She always thought she should have one especially for her.

As we got into the spring, I got a bike. This was one of Aunty Sarah's son's old ones and it had been in the barn for some time. Dad got it out and repaired it but the bike was a bit too big for me so Dad put some blocks on the pedals. Having a bike meant I was now chief errand boy and was even sent to pay money in at Lloyds bank in the town centre. The money was always pinned inside my jacket pocket with a safety pin and I always had a right job getting it out when I got to the bank.

Several of my friends had old bikes and we would go out for rides, I remember going to Sutton Park and one day we got to Lichfield. I looked forward to the day I would have the blocks taken off the pedals, but it never came! I was riding down the lane that led to the farm, which was always a bit bumpy when it happened. The bike just broke in half – it snapped off across the down frame and cross bar. No one had ever known this happen before but it was an old bike.

I was doing better at school these days. Old Patto taught us well and didn't stand any messing about but he was a fair old soul and we all seemed to get on well with him. He was like a lot of our teachers who should have retired but kept on due to all the young teachers being called up. Mother would give me a couple of eggs to take him occasionally although she always charged him a tanner for them. Old Patto was glad to get his hands on them since eggs was eggs and hard to come by.

We got a surprise one day as we came home from school; Mr Walwood's mare had a foal. The mare and her foal had been put in the meadow on their own. We kids soon made friends with it but had to be careful as the mare was a bit touchy and would soon swing round and kick you. She nearly got Bill one day but as she swung round to let Bill have both barrels he knew what she was up to and got out of the way quick.

Mr Walwood and his wife had a fish and chip shop in Dora Street and had taken the mare for a drive to Sutton Park on the Sunday night before it foaled, but the mare seemed to be all right and the foal was in top condition. The mystery was how she came to be in foal in the first place but Sid Perrins' horse Nelson finally got the blame, as he was the only entire horse in the field. However Mr Walwood seemed happy with his new foal and looked after it well since he knew a lot about horses as he had been in the cavalry during the First World War.

Mother's 'Dig for Victory' gardening didn't do to well this year as the novelty had now worn off. There were lots of other things to be done, like collecting pig food and looking after cows and pigs. With eight cows to be milked twice a day and pigs to be fed as well as Mother's milk round there was little time for much else. Ken was here Saturday afternoon and Sundays but Maisy always went home on Sunday to see her mother. A few rows got dug and some vegetables were planted but only about half the usual area was cultivated. Peas, beans along with turnips and beetroot were a must and Granny Mac's favourite parsnips, always pronounced by her 'pissnips' (much to our amusement) were planted. Cabbage was also planted mainly due to the Sunday muck collectors who would sometimes bring a few cabbage and broccoli plants for us. Granny liked her greens and would sometimes send Mary to collect a bit of sorrel for her to cook if we didn't have any cabbage. She also liked a few dandelion leaves on her salad in the spring. Mother was disappointed at not planting any potatoes this year as she had done well with last year's crop. They had lasted us all through the winter and Granddad George had scrounged a sack of them off Mother as well.

This year's must have for boys was a catapult or 'catty' but getting the elastic to make one was the main problem. Strips of motorcar inner tube were the usual material, but inner tubes were hard to find these days. We managed to steal an inner tube out of an aeroplane wheel one Saturday morning from a factory in Wallows Lane. The factory was called The British Optical Lens and had been repairing aircraft wheels for the last couple of years.

There was a public footpath to Bescot Station and Wood Green that ran behind this factory, which was fenced off with iron railings. All the old tyres and tubes were piled against these railings so it was a simple matter to pull one through. We picked a large tube, pulled it through the fence and made our escape over the level crossing, round the sewerage farm, into Bescot Road and through the park. Our next job was to get Y-shaped branches (forkies) from the hedgerows, the best of which were from the hazel tree in our garden. The leather for the sling part was easy as there a few old boots left by the last tenants in the barn. We cut the tongues out of the boots and they were ideal. Our catapults were supposed to be secret so we made them in our hut in the sand hole and buried our spare inner tube. We had enough to last us twenty years. We may as well have made them in the barn, as everyone knew we had them within half an hour. We used large pebbles for ammo that we got out of the sand, nice round ones about the size of a marble. The crows in the top of the elm trees around the meadow were now within the range of our cattys, as were the waterfowl on the pool. We used our cattys a lot but I never remember hitting any thing with them, still we tried.

Early in June 1944 we were woken one morning by a lot of aeroplanes flying over and some of them were quite low. Dad said they were towing gliders. We saw some ourselves when we were on our way to school. Something was happening but we didn't know what it was until much later in the day when it was announced by the B.B.C. that the allies had landed in Normandy and the invasion of Europe had started. There was great excitement and our parents were glued to the radio at every news bulletin. Most of the troops had crossed the channel in boats called landing craft, and stormed the beaches. Once a bridge head had been established a large concrete harbour, called Mulberry was towed across the channel. This was set up as a port on the French coast to keep the invading armies supplied; later a pipeline called Pluto was added to get motor fuel across the channel.

With all the excitement there was not a great deal done at school for the next few days and the invasion was all people could talk about for months.

We kids couldn't wait to get to the pictures to see the newsreels of the invasion. All the landing craft running up on to the beaches and troops and tanks pouring out was all a big adventure to us and very exiting.

Maisy's boyfriend was one of the soldiers involved so she had an anxious few days. She got a letter off him a few days later; he had made it without a scratch and that bucked Maisy up no end. Mother always reckoned Maisy was very unfair to her boyfriend, as she would go out chasing the Yanks down Walsall town most nights after milking. Very popular with the girls they were with plenty of money to spend. We kids liked to hear about Maisy's adventures down town and she would tells us all about it at breakfast. This often got Mother's goat, as far as she was concerned Maisy was a naughty girl but we kids thought she was great.

We broke up for the summer holidays and Mother found us some clothes that we could do what we liked in. She and Granny Mac had codged up some trousers for us out of an old coat someone had given Mother.

The summer saw us kids running wild as usual and if we were not collecting pig food we would be down the pool or in the park. As long as we were not causing a nuisance or damaging anything our parents just let us get on with it. If you could do it, Bill and I did it! Life was great, still is.

Granny went off to Devon to visit her sister for a fortnight and took Mary with her. Bill and I stayed home but we didn't get to Fradley this year, as Granddad George was not very well. He was eighty years old but he could still get a few pints of beer down him, especially if it was free.

Not being at school meant we could go with Dad in the cart to fetch the waste from the bakery and hospital. Our favourite trip was to Lichfield Market where Dad went to buy pigs on most Mondays. It was too far to go in the horse and cart so we would catch the bus to Lichfield and walk up to the market.

The thing I remember most when I think of these trips is of a man sowing a field of corn by hand. He was working in a field behind the Three Tunns Pub and had a large basket strapped to his waist with the seed in. As he walked along the rows he would broadcast a handful of seed to his right, and then to the left. We had seen pictures of farmers sowing seed by hand at school but this was the only time I ever saw it for real. It's always stuck in my memory over the years.

There were lots of distractions for us at the market once we knew how to work them and we could earn a couple of bob if we were lucky. One of the moves was to hang about outside the pub at the top of the market where they sold the cattle. A lot of the cattle buyers moved their animals by railway but the railway cattle pens were about half a mile down the road from the market. There were a couple of old drovers who took the animals to the pens as they were sold and this mostly worked well as the old cows were used to being handled. However, things were different when they got a pen of young heifers or bullocks to take across, as they were usually a bit wild and then the drovers would get a couple of us kids to help them. They always asked the buyer if they could use us but they always said yes. Our job was to chase after the cattle and stop them bolting off down the side streets on the way to the railway yard. The drovers were getting on a bit and were past the first flush of youth so couldn't chase after them if they escaped.

The buyer paid us each a shilling when we got back to the market and I think the drovers got half-a-crown each. You would never get rich doing it and I think I only did it a couple or three times since it wasn't worth the hanging about.

The large shed at the bottom end of the market was always a magnet to us, here they sold chickens, rabbits and all sorts of other small livestock. It was in this shed that Bill and I served our auction bidding apprenticeships. We bought a goat kid for half-a-crown one morning: this was our top bid, never any more. If we couldn't get it for half-a-crown we left it. Dad always encouraged us and would pay the bill, but had warned us two and a tanner was the limit. There were often young lambs for sale especially in the spring and one Monday we bought a couple of cade lambs (orphans). The ewe had rejected them or had died giving birth and the shepherd didn't want the bother of rearing them. I think we got them for a couple of bob and it was one of our best purchases. We had to feed them with milk for the first few weeks but we soon got them grazing. They were fully grown by the winter so Dad practised his butcher's skills on them so it made a change from pork. All the family got their lamb dinners and Old George got the fleeces tanned for hearthrugs. In future years we would look out for a couple of lambs and we always managed to buy some within our half-crown budget. The goat kid we only kept for a few weeks then sold it to one of our school friends, Albert Jones, for five bob. Bill and I would often make a few bob by buying rabbits and pigeons to sell on when we got home.

If Dad had bought any store pigs he would mark HP on the pig's backs with his red grease stick before arranging the transport home for them. Watts Transport who had an office in the auction yard was the firm Dad always used. Sometimes they would be delivered before we got home, but occasionally it might be nine o'clock at night before they came. The auction usually finished by about twelve thirty to one o'clock so we were back home by the early afternoon. This gave Dad time to do odd jobs before feeding the pigs and milking.

The summer holidays came to an end all too soon and Granny and Mary were back from Devon, Mary having adopted the accent of the area as usual. Someone had given her a day-old duckling to bring home that she named Sinobia and everyone was surprised it had survived the journey up from Devonshire. It only lasted a few days here; it fell into the drain by the dairy and drowned. Bill got it out of the drain and took it to Mary who wrapped it in some rag, held it up and was shouting, 'duckie, duckie, speak to me.' That gave Bill and me a titter. The burial service was held in the garden, Mary being the only mourner.

I was going up to the senior school when we started back at school and you could wear long trousers in the seniors. But, I would have to finish wearing out my short trousers before I got any long ones.

Things would be a lot different in the seniors; boys had a separate playground from the wenches. The boys could do all the normal playground games, but the wenches were not allowed to tuck their skirts up their knicker legs and do handstands up the wall any more as this was seen as not a nice thing for young ladies to do. It didn't stop some of them showing you their knickers in exchange for a bite of your apple or the apple core (known as the 'corkle').

The smoking room was in the corner of the playground, it was the boy's toilet and half the school would be in there having a crafty puff at playtime. It was all very clandestine or so we thought but the teachers would have had to be blind not to have seen the pall of smoke rising from it. They never seemed to bother about it. I think we only got raided once in the three years I was there and that was because Old Hobday probably had his arse in his hand over something.

To help the war effort the school kept some pigs and rabbits and these were on a strip of land at the back of Bescot Road. The senior school air-raid shelters had also been buried there and the ground on top used to grow vegetables.

I was in Titchy Brittel's class, named because he was only about five foot one but he was a nice little man. He was also the school sports master and a director of Walsall Football Club so if you played footie you were in with Titchy.

There were a lot of new faces in the class since kids from Edward Shelley and Palfrey junior schools joined us. The clever clogs of our junior school classes had gone to Edward Shelley or the Grammar School.

Although Titchy took us for most of our lessons we would have other teachers for some subjects; Gasser Guest for woodwork, Mr Bailey music and Aunty Hobday country dancing. That went down a bomb with us lads and we spent half our waking hours trying to think up ways of getting out of it. Volunteering to collect salvage was our main hope, but there were always more volunteers than the teacher would allow out of her class.

The autumn passed with the usual flurry of storing and preserving for the winter. I don't know why mother bothered; except for the jam a lot of it never got eaten. Doing it to help the war effort was Mother's view, a waste of time we thought. Probably the main reason was once we had bought the preserving jars we had to use them.

The farm must have been doing all right as Dad set another helper on. His name was Jacky Shutt and was the son of Mrs Shutt who kept the Chip shop in Narrow Lane. He had been working at Downs's farm on the Sutton Road for two years but Jacky was not very happy there as Old Downs was a bit of a slave driver so he was looking for another job. The problem was that due to the wartime direction of labour you were only allowed to move to the same or a similar job and needed permission to do so. Another factor was that Jacky was now sixteen and would be called up in a couple of years and Mrs Shutt didn't want Jacky to join the forces. The only way of escaping call-up was either by working on a farm or being a collier. However things got sorted out and Jacky came to work for us. With Jacky and Maisy and Ken at the weekend we were doing well.

Things were a bit different in the senior school at Christmas. We only had one day of entertainment before we broke up for the holiday. This was put on by the older classes and was mainly comedy sketches copied from Will Hay shows. Still we enjoyed it, as it was better than doing lessons.

At home we had the usual Christmas, although I can't recall much about this one except for Jacky and Maisy being off Christmas and Boxing Day which meant more work for Dad and Mom over the holiday.

Chapter Eleven

The New Year 1945 was let in as usual by our parents as they always were keen on it being done. They were both dark haired so it didn't matter which one did it, but it was Mother who let it in this year. Running through the house from the cold outside into the warm and back out into the cold would have made Dad cough and he did enough of that anyway.

Things were going well in the war and the allied armies were now on the German border. Everyone felt it was going to be a great year; even the street lighting in the town centre had been switched back on since last September and we had not had any air raids for some time. London seemed to be the target now and they had flying bombs and V2 rockets to deal with.

The bad news came a few weeks later when we heard that Billy Stone had been killed in action; this was a sad time but he wasn't alone. Some of the kids at school had lost brothers and fathers in the fighting, but life had to go on.

There was great excitement in March and it wasn't due to my twelfth birthday either!

We got a van, a Ford eight, second-hand of course from Reginald Tildesley the Ford dealer. It had been their delivery van but was now surplus to requirements. With Dad being on the list for a new one and with a wait of two years or more, he was offered it to tide him over until a new one became available. Petrol was very strictly rationed but being a farmer he would get a generous allowance of petrol coupons although the petrol Dad got contained a red dye, which stained the engine. This was to stop people using it in private cars.

Neither of my parents could drive but they were not going to let a small detail like that put them off. A chap named Johnson who was a Post Office van driver and used to fetch muck for his allotment gave them a couple of driving lessons in the yard on Sunday morning. Mom and Dad had already got their provisional licences so they stuck the L-plates on and drove the van. Dad was all right and soon learned. Mother took a bit longer and she never got above second gear for the first six months. I remember her going up the Broadway flat out in second gear – I thought the poor van would blow up.

We would have another driver later as Jacky would soon be old enough to get his licence. I don't recall what the rules were for learner drivers but both my parents just drove though they probably got away with it because there was a war on. Dad was the first to pass his test but it took Mother two goes to pass hers although she got there in the end.

The milk was now delivered in style, except for Monday mornings when Dad went to Lichfield Market in the van and Mother had to use her bike that day. Dad still had to use Watts to bring pigs home as the van would only hold two or three at best although it was alright for delivering a couple of pigs locally. Having a vehicle meant things like fetching the waste from the bakery and hospital took a lot less time and with Dad's chest he didn't have to drive the horse and cart in the cold and rain.

We now had no more use for poor old Harry, so he was taken to the Friday horse sale at Lichfield and we were all sad to see him go all except Mother who still had the bite marks on her neck where Harry had bitten her.

The wide strip of land between the farm and the railway was always a favourite place for courting couples and Mother was getting a little concerned it was getting too popular. The evidence would be left hanging on the railings every morning and she had always told us kids they were ducks' Wellington boots and never to touch them. We soon learnt different didn't we! Some of them had a knot in them and this we were reliably informed by the older kids, happened if the women crossed her legs while they were doing it. However there was little Mother could do about it other than going down the garden and looking over the fence all night. That was not an option as she would be branded a peeping tom and that would probably hit her milk sales. Dad suggested she put Ginky the goose out there, a large grey gander we had. Ginky had hatched on the morning of the allied invasion last year, the only one out of a sitting of goose eggs Dad bought from Lichfield Market. Ginky had been a pet when he was a gosling but since Christmas had turned a bit aggressive and would fly at anyone he didn't know. He got even worse when Dad bought a couple of geese to keep him company. Putting Ginky out there at night was decided against on the grounds that if the gander was outside of the farm and it was dark, he would probably end up on someone's dinner plate.

I was getting more merit marks at school these days but my writing and arithmetic were still pretty duff, although I always got very good marks in geography and history. Miss Chivers was the geography teacher; she was a young woman in her twenties and everyone seemed to like her. She would clear the kids out of the front desk at the start of the lesson and would then sit on it with her feet on the bench showing all her assets to the class. We always reckoned it could be the start of sex education classes.

On Friday afternoons the boys had woodwork and the wenches had a cookery class, an old buffer called Gasser Guest was our woodwork teacher. He had got the name Gasser due to him always having the glue pot bubbling on the gas burner ring. Every time someone came in the door the gas got blown out and we would have to suffer the smell until it got lit again.

A large cast iron treadle lathe was at the top of the woodwork class and everyone wanted a go on it but you had to be well in with Gasser Guest to even be considered. You had to supply your own large log of hardwood so that reduced the candidates even further but a wooden fruit bowl was the pièce de résistance usually turned on it by the selected few. Not many got to make a fruit bowl. I think there was only about three or four turned in the three years I was at the school.

Gordon Fenton who was Gasser's favourite turned the first one. Gordon's Dad was a carpenter by trade and in the dim and distant past Gasser had taught him during his apprenticeship, so Gordon was in!

By now we had done our learner pieces, a plant label and then a little tool holder so you could now choose to make something for home if you supplied the wood. Mother decided I should make her an ironing board and found a good thick plank of wood to make it with. The wood Mother gave me was dirty and greasy so Gasser made me scrape it clean before I could start. I got the school woodwork apron filthy and Gasser made me take it home to be washed so Mother was not best pleased. The ironing board project kept me busy until I left school and then I never completed it. One of the reasons I never finished it was because, if I had an errand to do for my parents it was always on a Friday afternoon. Missing woodwork would not damage my education, so they said.

My usual Friday afternoon errand was on the last Friday of every month when I would be sent to Wolverhampton to fetch milk filters. I would catch the train from Pleck station to Wolverhampton, walk down Pipers Row to Burgesses by the auction yards and collect four boxes of filters and bring them home. I had no trouble carrying them; they were only made of cotton wool. Bill finished making the ironing board; he had another two years to go after I left school.

As we got into spring one of our main interests was collecting birds' eggs. I became very keen along with one of my school friends Muggsy Fisher. Bill joined us for a while but soon lost interest, I think it was a clout of the ear off Mother that put him off. She caught Bill hanging over the roof of one of the barns. He was hanging on by his toes trying to get at a blue tit's nest in the wall. When Mother saw him up there we thought she was going to have a heart attack but by the time he had got down she had recovered enough to fetch Bill a clout round the ear.

Bill seemed more interested in fishing these days and Jimmy Ash was tutoring him on the finer points of angling.

Muggsy and I did all right but the egg-collecting season was only short and by July we would be wasting our time. We had been on a bird nesting expedition to Wood Green in early May and were on our way home (we had to be home by nine thirty). As we entered the park from Bescot Drive a woman in the garden of a house in the drive shouted to us that the war had finished. The only detail she had was from the wireless. When we got back home our parents confirmed all this and we were allowed to stay up late until ten thirty to listen for any further news. From this we learnt that Admiral Von Freidberg and General Hans Kinze had met Field Marshal Montgomery on Lunerberg Heath and surrendered the German northern armies to him. General Jodl, the German army commander would meet General Eisenhower later to sign a total surrender of all the German forces.

At school the next morning everyone was so excited that the teacher had a job keeping us in order. Old Hobday the headmaster turned school assembly into a bit of a thanksgiving ceremony and then we were given the day off and sent home. As we crossed the park on our way home we could see Dad had got the old bunting out of the loft and dressed the front of our house, it looked great.

Street parties were quickly arranged with people digging into their rations to make a few cakes and sandwiches. Mother got her old ice-cream tub out with a view to making some although it never happened because she couldn't get any ice. A bonfire was built at the bottom of Gower Street and we kids contributed by cutting up a dead Elm tree we had off the tip.

The B.B.C. announced that May the eighth would be known as V.E. day (Victory in Europe day) and for the next few days the country went mad! All the war effort now was put into seeing off the Japanese and this would come to an end sooner than we thought it would.

A bomb was tested in a desert in America and we saw pictures of a big mushroom-shaped cloud in the newspapers. They named it the Atom bomb and according to reports it had melted the sand and devastated the area for miles around. Japan was now threatened with having it dropped on them but they were not going to surrender that easily. The American air force dropped two Atom bombs on Japan in early August, one on Hiroshima and one on Nagasaki three days later. Japan surrendered and the government announced that day would be known as V.J. day.

This was during our school holidays, so we didn't get a day off but a thanksgiving ceremony for the end of the wars was arranged when we returned to school in the autumn. This was to be held in the two Churches in the Pleck. The first service was in the Methodist Church at the Brown Lion and the whole school was marched round there and lined up in Church. It was very musty in there and I started to cough and I couldn't stop myself, I was choking. One of the teachers, Aunty Hobday, took me outside into the fresh air but that didn't help a lot. The teacher took me into a little shop next to the Church and they gave me a glass of water, which helped. The next Church was St John's on Pleck Road but I wasn't allowed in there after my performance at the last Church. I had to wait outside with Aunty Hobday to see I didn't get up to any mischief.

A new distraction for us on our way to school was the building of prefabs on the field at the end of Slaters Lane. The council had now restarted their house building programme which been suspended for the hostilities and the men digging out the foundations were German prisoners of war but some of them spoke good English. We were fascinated with them and they were all very friendly with us kids. It was a surprise to find that they were not the Neanderthal degenerates the propaganda had led us to believe the German army was made up of. One of them even made our Mary a pair of miniature clogs and Mother gave Mary a packet of fags for him. They were only there for a couple of weeks and with the war ended they were probably due to be sent home. It was the only time we ever saw any Germans although there had been lots of Italian prisoners working on the railways around Walsall for most of the war. Like the Germans most of the Italians were very friendly and some married local girls after the war ended.

Things now seemed to be going well on the farm with Jacky and Maisy full-time and Ken appearing some weekends. Ken only came occasionally these days as he had other interests and he was due to be called up anytime now. I think he joined up himself, which gave you some choice of the regiment you could go in.

Things were going too well to last and the crunch came just before we broke up for our summer holidays. Granny Mac met us in the lane as we came home from school and ushered us into her room, you could cut the atmosphere with a knife. She gave us our tea and kept us with her until bedtime. All we could find out was Maisy was not with us anymore and we could hear Dad and Mom bawling at one another and doors banging. It would be much later that we found out what the trouble was. Mother had come back from delivering milk and had caught Dad and Maisy playing mommies and daddies in the cow shed. That made Mother's day I bet, she had marched Maisy to her room, made her pack her bags and chucked her off the farm!

Things quietened down after a few days because they had to; there was a farm to run. Dad though, was out of favour for much longer and he had to go to the British restaurant in the old church hall at the Brown Lion for his dinner. It all seemed to blow over in a couple of weeks and things soon got back to normal.

The surprise was that knowing what Mother was like when she was wound-up, Dad and Maisy were still alive!

Chapter Twelve

Now the war in Europe was over, a General Election was called and that got Granddad George out doing a bit of spouting. He had put up for the council as the Labour Party candidate for Caldmore on several occasions but without any success. Now Granddad was going to do all he could to support our local Labour candidate Major Wells. The old bugger was over the moon when he got elected and Labour formed the new government.

Bill and I got a week at Fradley with Granddad this year so Mother took Bill and me there in the van on Saturday evening after we had finished our pig food collecting. The van was only supposed to be used for farm business because that was what the petrol allowance was for so Mother put a couple of bales of hay in the back to make believe she was on farm business if she got stopped on the way.

I can't recall Gordon being at Granddad's hut this year; I think by this time he had left school and started work. He must have been there at the weekend because one of my abiding memories of this week is Gordon trying to buy an old air rifle off Ray Whittingham for ten bob. I can't remember if he got it though.

Uncle Gabriel's kids, our cousins, John and Valerie were staying with Mrs Keen for the week so we had their company. All we heard off John all week was 'cakey! cakey!' as this was all he ate. Aunty Gwen must have fed him on cake when he was at home but he had no chance of getting any with old George in charge! One day we were given half a pear each by the old major who lived with his sister in the house by the canal junction. Uncle Busty reckoned the Major must have had a funny turn if he had given us kids a half pear each.

We had a wonderful week running through the woods and paddling in the weir, Bill and I got on well with both of them and we had a great time together but it ended all too soon.

Dad came on Saturday night after milking to take us home; he had a quick pint in The Swan with his dad, sister Sarah, and Busty before we left Fradley for home.

Granny Mac was not at home when we got back from Fradley and mother said she had a breakdown and had gone to stay with Aunty Nan for a while. Mother would take us to visit her on Sunday afternoons and if it was a nice day we would sometimes meet her in Sutton Park. With Granny not living with us now, it meant a bit more work for Mother but with us kids being older we didn't need child minding any more.

One day during the school holidays we found a wooden stage floating in the pool. It was about four feet square and made of planks an inch thick. Someone had been trying to use it as a raft but when you stood on it, it sank. We fetched a wheelbarrow and took it back to the farm with a view to making it seaworthy. Dad had a pile of old five-gallon drums in the barn; they were old Cod liver oil drums (Dad occasionally gave the pigs a drop of it in their food). One drum was placed at each corner of the staging and fixed down with the bailing wire off the hay and the whole lot held down with fencing staples. We took it back down the pool, held a launching ceremony and it floated like a cork! Carl Jones was the first to try it out (well his dad was in the Merchant Navy). I think he took Masso Bird as a passenger with him.

The raft proved to be very tricky to handle and you had to keep it balanced or it tipped over. A few soakings were taken this day but we soon got used to handling it and now and again one of the drums would come loose but another couple of staples soon fixed it.

The top of the pool where the reeds grew was out of bounds to us as the swans still had their cygnets and would fly at us if we went near them, so we kept well away. It was hard enough balancing the raft without having to fight off cranky swans. If it was pouring with rain we still sailed it, well we were going to get wet anyway as we got tipped into the pool most times. In our minds we were always going somewhere on it, crossing the Atlantic or paddling up the Irrawaddy River as our imaginations ran wild. The only complaints we got were from the fishermen, 'spoiling their fishing' we were, or so they reckoned but they had the last laugh in the end. After we had gone back to school Jimmy Ash had taken our raft, cut the drums off and nailed it to some stumps he had knocked into the mud. This was along the line of reeds where he had tried to put the old cart. Jim had got his stage to fish off and he was a happy man, so the Bescot yachting club was now disbanded.

Bill and Mary joined me in the senior school after the holidays and I went into the second year. I would be in Mr Bailey's class, another old buffer who should have retired. We didn't have him for all our lessons, he was the art and music teacher. If he was taking a life drawing class, he would get one of the wenches to stand on a chair at the front. He would then explain the shape of the human body by feeling her legs and behind but he never got any complaints. You could see some of the wenches liked it, the dirty old man knew who to pick for his model.

Folk dancing was still the class to dodge if you could, so volunteering to collect salvage or pig food was the main escape route. Aunty Hobday was wise to this and only allowed four of us to miss the lesson otherwise she would only be left with the wenches. Bill and I were limited in our options as we could only volunteer to collect salvage. If we had ever gone pig food collecting for the school and Mother had found out we would both be dead. By the same token we were excused our turn at looking after the school pigs and rabbits but I think our Mary may have done a couple of weeks' rabbit keeping though.

The preserving of food for the winter was a bit slow this autumn, a bit of jam was made and a few eggs put down. Now Granny Mac wasn't here Mother didn't have time to do much so our Mary made the jam. Some of our pears were stewed and put in preserving jars but when we came to eat them some were all right but a lot had gone bad. Most of the apples kept all right wrapped in newspaper and stored on a bedroom floor.

With the war over we fondly thought things would soon get back to normal but we were in for a rude awakening.

The autumn saw the usual scrumping expedition and although there was plenty of fruit at home scrumped apples always tasted better. On our way from school one afternoon as we were going down Bescot Road we spotted a lovely apple tree in the back garden of a big house. This was next to a patch of spare ground so it was easy to get into the garden. There were four of us – Bill, me, and a couple of friends – but as we crept down the hedge at the side of the house Bill wouldn't come with us. When we got over the garden fence there were enough apples on the lawn, but we wanted to pick our own, didn't we. Our pockets were stuffed with apples and we were about to make our escape when a little Pomeranian dog came snapping and snarling down the garden followed by an irate woman. After we had got into the garden Bill had gone and knocked at her door and told her what we were doing. The lady made us empty our pockets while Bill stood there grinning; she even gave Bill one of the apples. A stern lecture was given to us about our behaviour and the consequences of it if we continued our life of crime. We all stood there looking very contrite and after vowing never to do such a thing again we were let off. Of course Bill got a pat on the head (the little squealer) but we gave him a thumping for twagging on us.

The pear harvest was a good one this year so we took some round the streets on our pig food collecting truck. Bill even sold some to Mrs Morris in Dora Street but I don't know how she would eat them as she had no teeth. Bill told her to suck them, that gave us all a giggle. The Sunday afternoon stall by the park did all right as well. If anyone bought five pounds of pears or more we delivered them free locally. Two pence a pound was all we charged, Mother had half the takings and the rest we kept for our pocket money.

It took us to the pictures on Saturday mornings and we had now joined the Gaumont Club at the Picture House in Walsall. It was dearer than the Forum, a tanner to go in but they had more Cowboy and Indian films on and occasionally there would be a Tarzan film too. They also sent you a card with a free entry for your birthday. Anyway, we couldn't get to the Forum most Saturday afternoons due to our pig food collecting.

At school we started to get some films on geography and history as part of our lessons and it was a change from looking up Miss Chivers' skirt. Mr Hobday the headmaster had borrowed the film camera off a friend for a trial and it was a great hit with us kids. Due to the success of the trial it was decided the school should have one of its own. Raffles were held to raise some money and film shows held after school for which we were charged two pence to watch. There was always a good crowd for the after school shows as old Hobday showed a lot of cartoons; he knew how to draw us in. However it took some time before enough money was raised for the school to buy its own cinematograph. Then it was only the one the school had borrowed in the first place.

The success of the films on history meant that we even got taken to the cinema one morning. The whole school was marched single file to the Savoy Picture House in Walsall to see the film, *Henry V*. Stern warnings as to our conduct had been given before we left school, no cheering when the 'baddies' were knocked of their horses. Watching the film in the cinema beat watching them in the school hall hands down; this was how lessons should be.

A couple of days before Christmas we had a bit of a scare with Bill and Mary. They had come home from school had their tea and then vanished. Mother sent me to look for them around the local streets on my old bike. I couldn't find them anywhere and I even went in the park searching although it was closed and there was no sign of them.

They both turned up at about eight thirty; Mary had taken Bill carol singing at the posh houses along the Bescot Road. Bill had a lovely singing voice and in fact Mr Voss the Pearl Insurance man had tried to recruit Bill for the Lichfield Cathedral choir. Bill wouldn't even consider joining any choir, as his life would have been misery at school if anyone found out he was a choirboy. They had done well from the carol singing expedition, which had earned them fifteen bob. This made the thumping they got off Mother for not telling her where they were going worthwhile. Mary had the money of course, but she shared it with Bill. She gave him five bob and kept ten bob herself.

There were no plays or sketches in the school hall before we broke up for the Christmas holidays this year. It was films instead. One of the films shown was the *Lost World*, but the dinosaurs in it frightened some of the kids, although most of us thought it was great and we all went home happy.

The joints of pork were distributed to the pig food savers in the usual secret operations during our collections. A lot of them had ordered fowl off us as well so we delivered them at the same time. It would make a better Christmas dinner than the whale meat now available at the butchers. Whale meat was not rationed so had become very popular although we never had any, but I think we tried whale sausage once and they were not too bad.

Santa came again to us; Bill got a set of fishing rods, Mary a tennis racket, me a new second-hand bike, (well I was chief errand boy). I helped Mother with the milk round on Christmas morning so she could cook a large dinner with all the trimmings. The Christmas pudding wouldn't flame though. The brandy Dad tipped on it had been in the cupboard for years and the alcohol had evaporated out of it so that was probably why it wouldn't burn.

Ken Taylor paid us a visit over the holiday, it was Guardsman Taylor now of The Coldstream Guards. He was on leave before being posted to Germany and we were all very pleased to see him and Mother gave him a couple of packets of her cigarettes before he left.

Chapter Thirteen

Early in the New Year 1946 Bill, Mary and I were sent by Mother to visit Granny Mac who was still staying with Aunty Nan at Sutton Coldfield.

It had snowed during the morning but only a couple of inches and Dad reckoned we wouldn't get any more. We set off after lunch taking some eggs and a little joint of bacon for Granny. While we were waiting for the Sutton bus it started to snow again fairly heavy, but all the buses seemed to be running so it didn't bother us.

The Sutton bus was a bit late coming but we caught it and set off. When we got to Aldridge the driver and conductor held a conference as to whether they should continue the journey. They decided to carry on to Sutton, although our Mary and a couple more people decided to go back to Walsall and got off the bus.

The bus got down the hill from Aldridge and across the Chester Road and was going through Little Aston when it ploughed into a snowdrift. The driver announced that was it, he was going no further and he would try to get the bus back to Walsall.

It had stopped snowing by now, so along with about a dozen other people we decided to walk the rest of the way to Sutton. Although it was only about another four miles to Nan's with the snow on the ground it felt like we were walking forever. However, we made it by about five thirty and were welcomed with open arms but I think it was the eggs and bacon that they were welcoming more than Bill and me!

Bill and I were given a hot drink and a couple of biscuits each (the biscuits were a treat) and plans were made to get us back home. Aunty Nan's husband Fred reckoned the trains would still be running and he should know as he worked for the L.M.S. Railway Company. It was nearly seven o'clock when Bill and I got to Sutton Station and the next train to Walsall was due at eight thirty. The waiting room was closed, there was no fire in it anyway and the booking clerk had probably used all the coal allowance to keep the booking office warm. To make matters worse the train never came till after nine o'clock so we both got monkey froze standing waiting on the platform. We got back to Walsall just in time to catch the last bus for Darlaston up to Gower Street and it was the first stroke of luck we had all day. Mother was in a bit of a state when we finally got home as to where we had been and why we hadn't we come back with Mary, but she soon recovered after a mug of tea and a couple of fags.

The bike Santa bought me was getting well used and Jimmy Ash was taking Bill on some fishing expeditions, but Mary would have to wait for the summer to use her racket. The racket had been bought on the promise that Mrs Thomas the school sports mistress would be introducing tennis lessons in the summer. It never came to pass though and Mary's only sporting chance came when Mrs Thomas made her goalkeeper of the hockey team. They were ten goals down when Mrs Thomas told Mary she was supposed to be stopping the ball going through the posts; Mary came home in tears.

None of us three kids were any good at sport. I thought I could swim but old Patto reckoned my hands were too small to make a fast swimmer so we were all a bit duff!

It didn't stop us playing all the games that came along and the Sunday afternoon football match was one of our favourites. The football pitches in the park were for official matches only; if old Walters the Park keeper saw us near them he would chase us off with his dog.

So, our football matches were held on rough ground at the bottom of the park, using our coats for goalposts. Games would start about two o'clock with probably four or five a side playing, and would build up during the afternoon as more came to join us. Sometimes we would have as many as twenty a side playing by mid afternoon. As we got towards teatime some of the players would start to drift away, but we kept on playing until there were not enough of us left to make the team up.

As the year progressed young men who had been demobbed from the forces took over the main pitches on Sunday afternoons. They didn't have football matches, they held football battles. After the pubs closed on Sunday lunchtime they would be down on the park sorting out who was playing who. It was supposed to be a friendly match but no prisoners were taken and each side played to win. Old

Walters never tried to stop them playing on the pitches as he would be risking life and limb if he ever tried.

One Sunday, a man and a couple of ladies from 'The Lord's Day Observance Society' did try to stop them playing football. No chance of that, but they should have been awarded the V.C. for even trying to stop that boozed-up gang crippling one another.

One of the tricks we would do if Old Walters was not about was to climb up one goalpost and go hand over hand along the crossbar and slide down the other post. Not many kids could do it, but Bill and I could! It was one of our party pieces.

It was now thought that because I had a bigger bike I could carry bigger loads so one afternoon I was sent to Walsall railway station to collect a hundred day-old chicks on it. Dad always had a hundred chicks every year from Chivers in Cambridgeshire. Why Dad or Mom couldn't have fetched them in the van I don't know. The chicks were in boxes of twenty-five, so I tied two boxes to each handlebar of my bike. As I was peddling home along the Wednesbury Road I met one of our schoolteachers, Miss Chivers. When she saw what I had and the name on the box she was very interested, so I opened a box to show her the chicks. When I got back home the chicks were perished and it was a good job Dad had got the brooder all warmed up ready for them. Another half an hour without any heat and half of them would have been dead.

On the Easter Monday Dad decided we were going horse racing at the Walsall races. After lunch we went with him and several of his Cronies in the van to the racecourse on Stencils Farm, which was off the Mellish Road. Mother and Mary were left at home to look after the farmyard.

There was already a good crowd there when we arrived and we only just made it in time to see the first race. Some of the races were for trotting horses and some for the gallopers; and there weren't many runners in some of the races, one had only two horses in it. With all the bookmakers there, Dad was in his element having a little punt on most of the races. Six o'clock was the last race and a horse named 'Dawn' won it, a horse named 'Sunset' was entered for it, but didn't run. Everyone reckoned it was a great afternoon out and Bill and I had certainly enjoyed it!

The pigs were all restless when we got back home since it was over an hour past their usual feeding time so we all mucked in and soon got them fed. Milking was half an hour behind schedule, but it was all done and ready by the time John Claridge came to collect it.

Train spotting was one of this year's main pastimes and a lot of our friends were doing it. The railway track on the far side of the park was one of the main lines to the north and always attracted a crowd of spotters in the early evening. They would wait on the fence by the signals for the expresses to come through and if the train had to stop at the signal it made their night. During school holidays and on weekends some would go train spotting to Trent Valley on their bikes. Bill and I were never very keen on it but we did go with them once but only got as far as Pipe Hill near Lichfield. Bill being a fisherman had stopped to check the canal that ran under the Lichfield Road there, so I stopped with him. While Bill was doing his feasibility study we noticed that a garden, which ran down to the canal, was a carpet of bluebells. The house itself was used for offices but I don't think anyone lived there, as most of the garden was overgrown. Bill and I must have spent an hour collecting the bluebells and we had a right pile to tie onto our bikes so instead of carrying onto Trent Valley we made our way back home. When we got there we tied the bluebells into little bundles with string and put them in a box. After we had eaten our tea we took them round the streets and tried to sell them a tanner a bunch. It was hard work and no one would buy, so we dropped them to three pence and still only sold a few. For all our hard work I think we may have made two bob between us.

Just as we thought things were going to get better it was announced that bread and flour would go on ration in July. It would be nine ounces a day for adults but I can't remember what we kids got. We never had bread rationing all through the war but apparently poor world wheat harvests in 1945 was the cause of it. Barley crops must also have been poor as many of the brewers were brewing low strength beer christened 'smackers' by the boozing fraternity. It was two pence a pint cheaper than normal beer but never very popular and soon died out.

Some imported fruit like oranges were coming in but they were very hard to get hold of. Mother did manage to fiddle us a crate of them from somewhere but they started to go mouldy before we could eat them all. The good news was that we were going to get another two pennies worth on our meat ration, not that it would bother us. Bread rationing didn't really affect us either, as we could always cadge a spare loaf off the bakery manager when we fetched the waste out of the Co-Op bakery.

Dad had always borrowed a bull to serve his cows or had taken them to one. It was now decided to have one of our own so Dad bought a young Friesian bull about two years old. He had some fancy pedigree name but he would be named Bill, the same as all bulls in the English-speaking world. He didn't have the ring in his nose yet so that was a job to do as all bulls had to have one by law. The ring was purchased from Burgesses and was about four inches in diameter, hinged in the middle with the opening end cut at an angle to make two sharp ends, and a screw to stop it opening once it was in the bull's nose. The ring came with what looked like a pair of bolt cutters, the ring fitted in the end of these and was used to force the sharp ends of the ring through the gristle in the middle of the animal's nose.

A Sunday afternoon was chosen as bull ringing day and Jeff Slater (now demobbed) along with Jacky would help Dad do it.

The bull was stood against the wall at the end of the barn where they had left out a brick about every couple of feet during the building of it. This was to allow air to circulate through the barn. Ropes were put around Bill's neck and body and passed through the holes in the barn wall. The rope round the neck was later changed to putting it on Bill's horns in case they strangled him. Bill was held firmly against the wall and Dad bodged the ring through his nose with the bolt cutter like tool. The bull didn't like it at all. I think it would be safe to say he was not a happy bunny. Getting the ring in the nose was the easy part but putting the little screw in to stop it coming out again would be a lot more difficult. After several attempts Dad gave up and Jeff had a go but he couldn't do it either. Jacky was the hero of the afternoon since he managed to get it in and screwed up tight. The gate to the field was opened, the bull untied and we all got out of the way while Bill made a bolt into the field. He would turn out to be a very different kettle of fish to the daft old thing Dad usually borrowed. The next time I was sent to fetch milk filters, I took the tool used to put the ring in the nose back to Burgesses and collected the deposit left on it.

Bird egg collecting was now in full swing again and this was carried out in the evenings after school. We even got captured and held for questioning by the Police one night. There were five of us and we had gone along Wood Green to Blackie's Wood at the back of Bescot Railway Sheds. On our way back we had just come through the railway arches and along the pool when two coppers jumped out of the bushes. They questioned us as to where we had been and what were we doing – bird nesting of course. Questions were asked as what each of our fathers did for a living and when Alfie Hale told them his dad was a major in the army I could see they were impressed. A stern warning as to our future conduct was given to us and we were sent on our way. Why we had been stopped in the first place, we couldn't figure out and we weren't going to push our luck by asking the Copper why.

Dad was over the moon on Derby Day because he had backed a horse called 'Airborne' and it had won. He wouldn't tell Mother how much he had won because she would then be able to work out much he had gambled on it. The winnings must have been considerable because Dad fetched them himself. The usual method of collection was for him to send Bill or me to the back door of the bookie's house with the message, 'anything for pigs'. Pigs was Dads betting nom de plume. He treated us all out of his winnings, giving us kids a pound each and Mother got a sealskin coat. But just as we were about to splash out on a spending spree with our pound, Mother made us all buy a fifteen-shilling saving certificate with it. The five bob left over was squandered on the pictures, loose women and drink.

Sammy Pearson the wholesale fruiter who had also run a fleet of coaches before the war now had his coaches returned. They had been requisitioned for military use by the government during the hostilities. To celebrate their return he was going to take Hilary Street School on a trip. Stratford upon Avon was chosen, as it would be a history lesson as well as a day out. At the morning assembly the day before the trip the Headmaster had given us a list of what we needed to take with us; some sandwiches and a drink.

On the morning of the trip we were lined up in the school playground and marched onto the coaches a class at a time. It was after ten o'clock when we set off and we gave a cheer to help us on our way.

When we arrived at Stratford we were put in a park by the river Avon, lined up by class and counted. I think the counting was to make sure no one had escaped on the way there.

It was nice in the park, the theatre was on the opposite bank of the Avon and we sat and had our sandwiches there.

After lunch we were split into two groups and one group put back on the coach. The other one was lined up and marched off over the bridge to visit Bill Shakespeare's house. Bill, Mary and I were all on the coach and we were taken to see Ann Hathaway's cottage on the outskirts of the town. The man in charge of the place gave us a talk on the history of it and how she became Shakespeare's wife. Before we came away Bill broke a chunk of old wood off from somewhere to keep as a souvenir. They would have murdered Bill if he had been caught. Back to the park for the change-over and it was now our turn to be marched over to see Bill Shakespeare's house. The curator gave us all a history of it and showed us round in small groups. Before we went back to the park we were taken to see the school where Bill Shakespeare had been a pupil.

At the park we were allowed half an hour to play before we were loaded up and taken for tea. Our food had been laid out in a large hut on trestle tables and was part of our treat. There was no chance of us overdoing it; half a lettuce leaf, a tomato and a slice of beetroot plus a dry bread roll, all washed down with a paper cup of weak orange juice. It was all free so we couldn't complain, could we?

All the coaches had followed each other when we were going to Stratford but they all went their own way coming back. Our coach was driving through West Bromwich on our way home when it ran over a dog. The driver stopped but nobody seemed bothered about the dog so he got back on the coach and drove back to school.

We were lined up in the playground and our names called to check no one had gone missing or had been left at Stratford before being sent home.

When we got back to our house Granny Mac was there, she had returned to live with us again. I think the having a breakdown story had been a smoke screen for leaving us last year. The real reason was that she had got out of the way for a while. It was probably Granny who had twagged on Dad and Maisy's 'cow shed capers'.

Dad's next problem came at the end of June one Saturday morning; he had just finished milking and feeding the pigs and had settled down to read the *Walsall Observer*. Dad had been reading for some time when he suddenly shouted Mother to come. He had spotted an advert placed by The General Hospital and they were asking interested people to bid for their kitchen waste. Dad was purple with rage, he had fetched it when nobody else would and they couldn't do it! He would see the Matron.

The Matron was very apologetic and she didn't think it was right, (she could see her occasional free eggs going down the plughole) but it was a hospital management decision. Dad made a bid but it was not enough so he didn't get it. We would miss the cutlery out of it but we had collected enough to last a lifetime over the years.

Chapter Fourteen

The school holidays started at the end of July and Bill and I would have our week at Fradley. We would not be stopping with Granddad this year as he was not very well and didn't come to Fradley anymore. Our accommodation for the week was a large bell tent next to Uncle Busty's hut with two double beds. Bill and I slept in one and the Mattocks brothers slept in the other. The Mattocks brothers were both deaf and dumb but were about the same age as us, so we got along very well with them. Their father Sid and Uncle Busty slept in the hut and did the cooking. I can't remember what the food was like but it must have been alright, mind you we would have eaten anything in those days. Some nights after our meal Mrs Keen would come round with some cake for us kids and we looked forward to that! We all had a great week; we even did some fishing with proper fishing rods. Sid and Uncle Busty would fish in the mornings until The Swan pub opened. After their lunchtime pub session they would retire to the hut for a nap, leaving their rods propped against the hut. While they were snoring their heads off we would borrow the rods and do a bit of fishing. They never woke before about five in the evening so we would get a good three hours' fishing.

While we were there a lot of the barges coming down the canal were carrying wheat and Uncle Busty had won a couple of sacks off them during the week. When Mother came with the van to pick us up on Saturday night, she got the job of taking it back to Aunty Sarah's in Shelfield on our way home.

While we had been at Fradley Mary had holidayed in Blackpool with one of her school friends, Doreen Healey and her parents. It seems that this made her a better person than Bill or me (well we hadn't stayed in a hotel, had we). She must have had a good time because we never stopped hearing all about it for months.

The pool was always one of our main playgrounds during the holidays and we spent a lot of our time down there. It was there on a summer's evening at about seven thirty that our bull Bill got his first victim. Dolly Gregory, who had left our school and now had a job, came parading round the pool done up like a prize terrier in her mother's high-heeled shoes. Bill the bull and the cows were grazing by the pool and as she walked past, the bull just lifted his head and looked at Dolly. I don't think Bill intended to charge her, he was just watching but Dolly took fright and dashed into the pool leaving her shoes stuck in the mud. Dolly made it across the pool and over the railway fence on the other side to safety. It took a while to rescue her shoes as we couldn't stop laughing for half an hour.

Another good laugh was watching Jimmy Ash chasing the heron who was having the fish out of the pool; Jim considered these were his. Jim would borrow Dad's old twelve bore shotgun and wait behind the little bridge by the railway. He hunted it all summer and never even got a shot at the bird, if Jim was at one end of the pool the heron would be at the other and it probably died of old age in the end.

On Monday mornings we liked to go to Lichfield Market with Dad in the van. We always had a good couple of hours there making the odd bid if we fancied anything. During the late summer there were always a pile of boxes of day-old chicks, they were mainly Cockerels and surplus from the hatcheries. The auctioneer would put up the first box and it would probably make three pence or up to a tanner on a good day. He then sold off the other boxes to anyone who wanted them at that price. There were twenty-five chicks to a box and you took pot luck as to how many of them would be alive. The trick was to wait until all the boxes on the outside of the pile were sold, as these would be cold and most of the chicks dead. Boxes in the middle of the pile would be a lot warmer so most of the chicks were alive. If we bought a box we would put them in Dad's brooder to warm up when we got home and then sell them off for three pence each. People would put them in a box on the hearth to keep them warm until they were old enough to go outside (about four weeks) and fatten them for Christmas.

Saturday afternoons were still reserved for pig food collecting but now we only collected around Dickinson Drive. Since losing the hospital waste Dad was buying stock feed potatoes from Hydes at Stonnall. They were arable farmers and had always fetched our pig and cow muck to use on their fields and Dad had bought his hay and straw off them for a long while.

One of our main projects during the holiday was an aerial ropeway from a tree in the garden that ran across to the field barn. The wire rope was given to us by the railway workmen one morning when they were renewing the cable that worked the signals. They let us have a length just long enough to tie around a tree on the edge of the garden and on to an old windlass in the loft of the barn. The windlass was very old and must have been used to haul things up to store in the loft in years gone by, but it still worked. The rope was put through the window next to the windlass and wound up tight. We raided Dad's workshop and found a little pulley to put on the wire with about two feet of rope with a dustbin lid tied on the end to hang off the pulley. The dustbin lid was for us sit on to ride down. I think we got the angle of the wire a bit too steep as we hit the tree with some force; the bin lid would hit the tree and tip you on the floor if you didn't hold onto the rope tightly. However we soon got the hang of it and found that twisting the pulley as we went down slowed it up a bit. It wasn't long before we were launching ourselves out of the window hanging on to old meat hooks, bucket handles, and anything we could hang on to and slide down the rope. If you went down on a hook you needed to drop off before you reached the tree or else you got a right wallop when you hit it. Like all good things it came to an end all too soon, but it had lasted nearly a month. Dad had a load of hay delivered and as the lorry was backing up to get in the yard it caught the wire rope. It didn't break the rope but pulled the old windlass off the wall in the loft and we could never get the rope taught enough after that to be any good for us to slide down.

Since Granny Mac had been back in residence she and Mary were back on the God Shop run and Mary had been roped in to join the Girl Guides who met in the church hall. So it was now decided by Granny and Mother (we never found out why) that Bill and I would benefit from being Boy Scouts. The local Scout troop met on Wednesday evenings in the Wesleyan Hall on the Bescot Road, so Bill and I were scrubbed-up and sent off to join them. The Scoutmaster was a local government 'bigwig' and most of his troop were the sons of gentlemen, so a couple of rag-arsed cowboys like us were not the sort of recruits he was looking for. He put us on a month's trial to see if we would fit in and if we did we would be sworn in. You could see he didn't want us in his troop – that was very plain. However, this proved to be our first and only meeting as Bill got us drummed out before we got in! On our way home down Slater's Lane, Bill had chalked 'be repaired' (the scout's motto 'Be Prepared') on the wall of Scribbens Bakery. Someone saw him do it and must have twagged on Bill because when we went to the next Scout meeting we were promptly shown the door. Mary was more successful with the Guides; she did get to go for a couple of weekend camps at Beaudeseart with them.

This year's scrumping disaster was also in Slater's Lane at Granny Worth's, who kept a frowsty little shop in Sheridan Street. Granny Worth was a nice old dear; we could always buy our fags off her with no questions asked. Bill used to go and do some odd jobs for her occasionally (always into helping old ladies was our Bill, still is). A row of apple trees ran down the middle of her garden, which was separated from the lane by a four-foot high wall. We should have checked to see if anyone was coming down Sheridan Street before we shinned over the wall. The apples were no good anyway, all full of Codling moth grubs. As we turned to go back over the wall, there looking at us were the local beat Bobbies, Sergeant Harris and a Constable. There was no escape; Jimmy Harris was a friend of my parents and was a regular member of the Sunday morning conference gang in our yard. We shinned back over the wall and just as I had landed on the other side, Jimmy Harris stuck his boot up my backside with some force. Georgie Burgoyne got a whack with the Constable's cape before we could run away. The kick up the jotter must have been the cure for scrumping as I never did it again until I scrumped a couple of figs from a tree in Greece forty years later.

It turned out to be a bad week because my next trick was to fall out of a conker tree in the Rookery. I fell on my head, it was a good job it had been raining and the ground soft but I was still concussed and had to be taken home. Granny Mac wrapped my head with warm brown paper and sent me to bed. The brown paper treatment must have worked because I was as right as rain by the morning.

Mother came home from her milk round one morning, full of herself. She had been delivering in Slaney Road when no lesser person than Harmer Nichols, chairman of Darlaston U.D.C. had stopped her and asked if she would deliver to his house. Could she just! Mother, always looking to do a bit of social climbing, would be only too happy to deliver a couple of pints of milk and a gallon of diffidence each and every morning. With Councillor Stanley Evans a customer in the same road, Mother thought she had hit the big time, there was no holding her. Clothing coupons were squandered on buying a white overall from the Beehive for her to wear while delivering the milk. Dad offered to paint 'by appointment' on her milk can but she didn't take the offer up.

All too soon it was time to start back to school for my last year. There had been some building going on while we had been on our summer holiday. A large room had been put up on the strip of ground that ran along the side of the school. Rumours abounded as to what it was for and we were soon to find out. On our first morning assembly and after Old Hobday had taken prayers we sang the hymn 'When a Knight Won His Spurs in the Stories of Old', a new teacher was introduced to the school, a Miss Williams who was going to be the head of English teaching. Then the announcement was made; the school in future would be known as 'Hilary Street Secondary Modern School' and the new building would be a dinning room. The new dinning hall was well sited at the top end of the strip with the pigs at the other end. School dinners would be available in the near future and printed details of these would be given for us to take for our parents. Hobday then issued his annual threat of the dire consequences of being caught using a pea shooter at school. We took no notice and still did; there was always plenty of ammo, usually hawthorn berries at this time of the year. The school then marched out of the assembly to Old Bailey thumping out 'Blaze Away' on the school piano.

I was in Dickey Lambert's class now and he was another old buffer who should have been long retired. Dickey was the school head of science, such as it was at Hilary Street. Our classroom was the other wooden one next to Mr Bailey's class and the ceiling bristled with pen nib darts that had been flicked up there over the years. It was supposed to be the science lab but there was only a bench along the back of the class with a couple of gas taps and a sink. While we were in the class one of the gas taps and the sink were in constant use. Dickey had set up a still on there making distilled water and he must have made enough to top-up every car battery in Walsall.

One of our first science lessons with him always sticks in my mind. Dickey had set up a flask of water coloured with red ink, a bung in the top and about two feet of glass tube sticking out of the bung. A Bunsen burner was placed under the flask and as Dickey turned the heat up or down the water went up and down the tube. This experiment was to show us how things expanded when hot and contracted as they cooled. He was warming it up for the third rise up the tube when the whole lot exploded showering the front row of the class with coloured water. That gave us all a bit of a giggle. Luckily no one got cut by the glass and Mr Thomas the caretaker was sent for to clean up the mess.

English lessons with Miss Williams proved to be a bit of a struggle for she was a lady on a mission. As well as teaching us the mysteries of written English she was also going to teach us to speak proper. She would have the class reciting a poem, 'I wish I lived in a caravan with a horse to drive like a Peddler man, he has a wife and baby brown and on they go from town to town'. He must have been a posh Peddler man to have a horse, as we only had 'osses' around here. Our pronunciation was to be changed from Black Country to B.B.C. spoken English and wenches would be called girls in future. She had no chance. As soon has we left her class most of us would be back to speaking normal. Some of the wenches (sorry, girls) started talking a bit posh, but half the class was only semi literate anyway.

Chapter Fifteen

The pear harvest in 1946 was good this year and we made a bit of pocket money selling them by the park fence. Granny bottled a few again for the winter, the pears and a few jars of jam were all that was saved this year.

A lot of things were now harder to get than they had been during the war. Mother's cigarettes were one of them and a lot of Turkish cigarettes were now on sale like Clifton and Pasha. They were terrible to smoke and smelt even worse. No one wanted to smoke them so the shopkeepers would only sell you ten Virginia cigarettes if you bought five Turkish off them, just to get rid of them. Mother did manage to keep a supply coming with a few well-placed eggs and a bit of bacon in the right places.

As the weather got colder fuel for the fires became very short and a lot of people took to digging their own at Bentley. The coal up there was near the surface and they would go digging at the weekends and cart it home in anything that would carry it. The queues for coke at the gasworks on Saturday would snake along Prince Street and up the Pleck Road as far as Walker Bros.

We did alright for coal due to one of Aunty Sarah's sons, Douglas. Since being demobbed he was working for a haulage firm driving a tipper lorry delivering coal to local power stations. If he was quick lowering the back of his lorry when he delivered the coal to the power station there was always a few hundredweight left on the lorry. Doug would bring it and tip it on the heap in our yard by Dad's boiler. It was mainly slack he brought but it kept the pig food boiler going, the house fire burning all night and the two large kettles of water on the hob hot.

The problems with the shortages were that people were being demobbed and finding jobs. They had a lot of money and nothing to spend it on. A motorcar was what everyone wanted but there was a two or three year waiting list for a new one. The factories had now turned back from war production to making cars and vans, but they were all for export. 'Export or die' was the slogan of the day now. Second-hand motors sold for more than they cost new.

Jacky, Dad's helper came with one his mother had bought him for his birthday; well he wouldn't get one on the money Dad paid him. It was an old 1930 Morris with big brass door handles and it broke down every couple of miles but Jacky was happy with it, although to everyone else it was a bit of a laugh. When Jacky came with the Morris car it was a surprise to us all as he had been looking at Tom Perry's old Clyno with a view to buying that. The Clyno was more in Jacky and his dad's line as they had a back yard full of old motorbikes and things that didn't work. They were always just on the verge of getting them all working but never quite made it. Jacky had bought Dad's old horse-drawn float and the harness but never got a horse.

There were more vehicles on the road now as the Government was selling off the old army motors at auctions. They were mainly commercial vehicles but a few were American left-hand drive station wagons that only did about twelve or fifteen miles to the gallon and with petrol still strictly rationed those who bought them never got very far in them.

Horses were still king of the road for the time being and fetching good money at the sales. Harry Titley, Jackie's cousin had been to the Welsh pony sales and bought a wild one for a fiver at the autumn round-up sales. Harry had broken the pony in and made a little cart for it – he had a nice little turnout when he had finished. He earned a few bob with it delivering five bob loads of muck to the allotments on Sunday mornings and it paid for the pony's keep. Harry was a busy young man. As well as working full-time at the Co-Op stables he also looked after Herbert Field's pair of show hackneys. He would sometimes bring them down our yard when he was exercising them, two lovely high stepping black horses, one named George and the other called Misty. Our Bill was very taken with them and they were probably the start of Bill's lifelong interest in horses.

There were a couple of racehorses that came occasionally and Dad allowed them to canter around the edge of the top field. They belonged to Dawson's, a haulage contractor who had a garage on Pleck Road. I don't think they ever won any races but Old Dawson was happy with them.

Bill and I now became interested in guns. What had started us off was finding an old Diana air pistol that had been left by one of the soldiers when they where camped on our field. We had been mooching in the large cupboard at the bottom of the stairs when we found it on a top shelf. We tried to keep it secret but when Mary knew she soon twagged on us. We were allowed to keep it and although Mother was not too happy with us having it Dad reckoned it was time for us to learn how to use one. He wasn't going to let us loose with his old twelve bore but Dad had a little six millimetre bore rifle as well. The trouble was the rifle had been made in Germany and there was no ammunition available for it, but Dad had a plan!

As I finished school the following day I was to peddle my bike down Walsall to Shuffery's in Digbeth and purchase a little rat-tail file for him. The breach of the rifle was filed out a bit and allowed a point two-two to fit in if you shaved a bit off the lead bullet first. Dad tried it out and it fired alright; the bullet went through the living room door and lodged in the door behind it. No way was Mother going to let us play with that!

We had to make do with the Diana pistol until one Sunday morning a couple of weeks later. Armed with a copy of *The Walsall Observer* 'for sale' pages, Dad got Bill and me in the van and took us to a house in Bentley that had some air rifles for sale. They had several rifles and Dad tried them all. Bill and I had a go with a couple of them and we did alright, we hit the target! After a bit of bargaining we ended up with a Lincoln Jeffries .177 air rifle for Bill and I to share; it was a bit large and it was all we could do to cock it, but we managed. We had a whale of a time for the next few weeks shooting rats and knocking sparrows off the drain spouting. Teddy Dukes complained to Dad about us shooting the rats in the old wall down the pig field on the grounds that we were spoiling his Sunday morning ferreting expeditions, he enjoyed his bit of ferreting did Ted. However there were enough rats in that wall to keep us all busy.

As the days drew in and it got dark earlier we kids were allowed to play out later since streetlights were starting to be put on again. The lights in the town centre had been on since the autumn of 1944 but they were electric. Lights in the outlying districts of town were still gas. The tops had been taken off when the war started and these all had to be replaced before they could be turned back on although most streets had the lights back on by now.

One of our favourite games to play in the dark was 'release' in which half the kids playing would go and hide. The rest of us would go and search for them and if found they would be put in the den with a couple of us left to guard them. If one of the kids hiding could sneak back to the den without one of the guards touching him and touch the prisoner and shout 'release' he was free to go and hide again. Kick the can was another game very similar in which the idea was to avoid the guards and kick the can.

Saturday nights we would amuse ourselves at the bus stop on the Darlaston Road. We had some old German money that Ken Taylor had given us and one of the notes looked like an English ten-shilling note. The bus shelter backed onto the canal bank and had a gap of about a foot all round the bottom of it. We tied some cotton on the note and put it on the floor of the shelter and stationed ourselves at the gap at the back. When someone came for the bus and spotted the note they would try to pick it up. A tug on the cotton pulled it just out of their reach. If someone got a bit nasty we escaped down the canal bank, but most of them saw the funny side of it. A couple of weeks' fun was had with the note until a woman (who we must have had before) stood on the cotton while picking the note up. She gave the note back but ripped it in half before she did, so that was the end of that little game. By now it was getting too cold to lie on the ground at the back of the bus shelter anyway.

Bonfire night 1946 was back again. Bonfires had been banned during the war and fireworks were very hard to get. Colin Thorpe (Polly Dope to us kids, because he was always making and flying model aeroplanes and dope was what he painted them with) was fetching a few from somewhere in Brum and flogging them at a profit, he was also making a few fireworks himself to sell.

We only bought a few bangers off him as he was very expensive, so we made some fizzers ourselves with sulphur, saltpeter, charcoal and iron filings. Bangers were the favourite and we did try to make some but we never managed to. There was not much about to make a bonfire with so we didn't have a very big one. Spuds were stuck on lengths of wire and put in the fire to roast and although they were only half cooked when we got them out we still ate them.

As we got towards the year end things seemed to be going well on the farm, but like all farmers to Dad it had been the worst year in living memory. Mother was doing alright with her milk round and with us kids being older we could do some of the evening deliveries on our own which helped her a lot. Coopers grocer's shop in Dickinson Drive was our favourite delivery. If old Cooper had any sweets he would always give us a couple when we took his milk.

The orders for chickens for Christmas dinner got messed up when Jacky came one morning and asked if his Mother could have a dozen of Dad's fowl. She had orders for them from her chip shop customers and someone had stolen hers last night. It all turned into a bit of a laugh as the pen they were kept in was right at the back of the Brown Lion Police box. The thieves had spent some time sawing though the padlock to get in the pen although the door was only held on with leather hinges, a typical Old Man Shutt construction. Dad fixed her up with some fowl but kept them for her until Christmas Eve.

Mother decided to cheer us all up for Christmas by falling out with Granddad George. They never did see eye to eye, they were political opposites and like most of George's daughters-in-law, she was not a member of his fan club. The government had passed some bills during the year like the National Insurance Act and we are going to have a National Health Service as well. It would take another eighteen months before that came in, it took that long for the Government and Aneurin Bevin to convince the medical profession it was what every civilised country should have; not a Communist plot as portrayed by some of the press.

Old George was over the moon with it since he had spent most of his life fighting for such things. Mother was not convinced, in her view if you were sick or out of work it was your problem not the government's. There were no deserving poor in Mother's book and she claimed the cure for most illnesses was to give the patient a sharp slap of the face and tell them to pull themselves together.

The usual Christmas fowl and pork deliveries took place as we collected the kitchen waste, well it was expected now. Dad with the help of Jeff Slater had slaughtered a couple of extra pigs for the black market so they would make him some cash. He must have done alright as on the Saturday before Christmas I was taken to the 'Weaver to Wearer' shop in Wednesbury. Clothing coupons were splashed out on a new suit for me with long trousers. I had worn long trousers for a couple of years but these were the first shop ones I had. All our long trousers we had before had been made for us by Mother or Granny on the old sewing machine. Bill and Mary got new coats and they were our gifts from Santa.

Mon and Dad had just gone to bed on Christmas Eve when they heard someone creeping about downstairs. It was the creaking of the dairy door opening that woke them. Dad went down with his old twelve-bore shotgun to find our Mary in the yard. Some fool had told her that all cattle kneel down on their front legs at midnight on Christmas Eve so our Mary had gone to the cowshed to see if they did. She was to be disappointed. Bill helped Dad with the milking on Christmas day.

Chapter Sixteen

The New Year 1947 was let in as usual but this year there was a choice of carrot or elderberry wine. It was difficult to choose as we didn't get enough to taste and we needed more to warm us up as the weather had turned bitter cold.

It was all change when we got back to school after the holiday. On our first school assembly we were introduced to a couple of new teachers, Mr Penal and a Miss Thornley. Dickey Lambert had finally retired along with a lot of old teachers who had been kept working during the war. When we found Mr Penal was to be the replacement for Dickey and our teacher, we nearly weed ourselves with excitement. He had been a navigator in a bomber during the war and we lads knew all about bomber raids through reading the exploits of Flight Sergeant Braddock in the Wizard every week. Lessons became a lot more fun with him teaching us, especially when he was telling us about the stars and sky. I was always interested, as like Granddad Mac, he was able to navigate by the stars. Mr Penal had been taught this skill while serving with the Air Force, however it wasn't to last long for me as this was my last term at school; mind you, anything would have been a relief after Dickey.

A new lesson was added called 'current affairs' in which the class was encouraged to discuss the news of the day. It was only one lesson for half an hour a week but everyone was keen on it. Some of the class was even sneaking in the Council reading room in the Pleck for a look at the papers on their way to school. Discussions were always very lively and got a bit heated at times and we loved it – why couldn't we have had something like this before?

It was a bitter cold January with some snow and the coldest since eighteen fish and chips or something like that. Dad was struggling with the farm as some nights the temperatures fell twenty degrees below. The pigs were getting two hot meals a day as normal but now had an extra hot meal on a Sunday evening. Dad had always given them one good feed on Sunday morning and not fed them again till Monday morning.

The milk yield off some of the cows was a bit down but not entirely due to the cold. Since her Christmas performance our Mary had given herself the job of feeding the cows, a sort of 'apprentice milkmaid' (probably still waiting to see if the cows were going to kneel down). Dairy nuts were fed in strict measures (according to how much milk each cow was giving) at milking time and this was when Fanny did the feeding. She was giving extra nuts to the cows she liked and less to the cows she didn't like. When Dad caught her doing it he banned her from the cowshed – her milkmaid career in tatters. 'I'm not having her fannying about with the cow's rations' Dad said. After that everyone was calling Mary 'Fanny' and the name stuck although she didn't mind as she thought Fanny Power sounded better and more up-market than Mary Power.

Mother was always on time with her milk deliveries in spite of the snow. She had suspended the evening deliveries and with the weather being so cold the milk would keep for a couple of days but we kids found it a bit thin collecting pig food. Most of it was frozen solid in the buckets and we had to knock it out. We had our little fire cans to get warm when we were playing in the yard but we couldn't take them with us pig-food collecting in case we set the van on fire.

Dad was struggling with his chest and coughing his lungs up. The goose fat and warm pads administered by Mother didn't seem to help him much. With this and the weather, Bill and I had to help Dad with the farm so we missed a lot of our schooling. As a result Mr Hubble the School Board man came after us. We spotted him one afternoon limping down Gower Street, a big man in a long black overcoat and homburg hat. Bill had a plan – he drove Ginky the gander and his geese round into the drive. As Old Hubble got through the gate Ginky flew at him, that soon saw the back of him! We expected to be in trouble when we did get back to school but nothing was ever mentioned about it.

Not much fun was to be had on the ice this year, two or three days was all we got as the snow was too deep. February turned out to be worse than January, we had more snow. There were deep drifts everywhere and it snowed on twenty-six consecutive days. The Town Council had a lot of the men being demobbed from the forces to help clear it off the roads. The Power Stations couldn't supply enough electric so there were power cuts all the while. This was where we were lucky still being on the gas supply and although the pressure was a bit low at times we never got cut off. It was March before the thaw started and with the ground still being frozen it couldn't soak away. There were floods everywhere.

To try and even out the electric supply the government altered the working week by having a half day off in the week and working weekends. The normal working week was Monday to Friday and Saturday morning. Now some of the factories would have half a day off in the week and work Saturday afternoon or Sunday to make up for it, this half day off in the week was always known by the people doing it as their 'Spiv day'. Even with this there were still power cuts.

About the middle of March we had a surprise when we got home from school for lunch, or dinner as we always called it. There, parked outside our dairy and gleaming in the sun was our new Ford Van, KDH 999. It was painted dark blue with H. & J. Power, Bescot Farm written on the side doors. Dad had a removable partition fitted behind the front seats for when he was carrying pigs. You wouldn't want them in the passenger seat telling you where to go would you?

Bill and I just had to have a sit in it and this led to a punch-up of who was going sit in the driver's seat. The receipt for the van was still on the dashboard, it was two hundred and five pounds, twelve and six pence.

I got my first ride in it a few days later to help Jacky fetch a young boar from the station. Dad had bought a Middle White boar from a breeder in Yorkshire; Colton Vanguard was the pig's pedigree name. The Post Office telegraph boy had delivered a telegram to tell Dad the pig was expected to be at Walsall goods depot at six thirty this evening. This was the cows' milking time, so while Dad carried on with the milking I was sent to help Jacky collect the pig. They always came in a wooden crate with little cast-iron wheels on so you could push them around. The crates had to be returned or you would be charged for them so we normally put the crate up to the van and got the pig into the back of van and sent the crate straight back.

Jacky and I got to the goods depot in Station Street just as it was getting dark to be met at the door by the parcel clerk, the front his waist-coat brown with snuff stains. We could see he in was in a bit of a tizzy. 'They're over in the corner,' he told us, but we were only there for one pig. When we got to the far corner of the depot there were two goats and he had used the pig crate to help pen them in. They had string round their necks where the address labels had been, but goats doing what goats do had eaten them. They had taken a chew at some of the parcels as well and that's what got the clerk in a tizzy. There was no way of telling who they belonged to; they had probably come down the main line into Brum. The goods depot there, seeing them with no labels on had sent them on to Walsall with the pig just to get rid of them. Jacky and I got the pig loaded up and the clerk tried to get us to take the goats but we told him to go down the road to the railway stables and get them some hay to chew on.

Dad advertised our old van in the *Walsall Observer* and had several buyers turn up. The first people to see it bought it and after two years' wear out of it, Dad almost got back the same money he had paid for it.

Friday the fourth of April 1947 was my last day at school but there would be no leaving ceremony, just an announcement in the morning assembly.

For all those without jobs the Labour Exchange in Wednesbury Road was opening a school leavers' jobs office in the morning. The rush was for jobs with the Co-Op laundry as they paid the best wages by far at twenty-eight bob a week. Only about half the class left at Easter, all the rest would stay until the age of fifteen. Kids born before Easter 1933 like me would be the last to finish school at fourteen.

I thought I would be working for Dad but Mother had other ideas; I had got to learn a trade. This didn't surprise me as I had suspected for some time Mother had fallen out of love with farming. There was a right argument in the dairy between my parents about my not working for my father. This was the first time I ever heard my Dad use foul language.

Mother got her way and I was taken to the Beehive and togged out in a new boiler suit ready for my career in industry…

I was allowed the Easter week to run wild before I had to learn a trade, as Mother would put it.

The weather was still a bit cool so we were still swinging our fire cans. We were swinging our cans down by the old air-raid shelter at the bottom of Gower Street one afternoon when Polly Dope came to see us. He had been making stink bombs and had some powder in a tin can. Polly set light to the powder and told our Bill to have a good sniff – it took Bill's breath away. We dragged Bill back home coughing and choking, he was in a bit of a state. When Mother saw him she sat Bill in a chair and gave him some milk which seemed to calm him down and help him breathe better. As soon as Bill had recovered a bit Mother got on her bike and was off after Polly, but of course he had vanished by now. His mother, Mrs Thorpe, was after him as well; it seems he had stunk the house out with his experiments. Mrs Thorpe assured Mother she could leave it to her to deal with Polly when he came home. Bill soon recovered from his ordeal and later that week he would meet a new friend.

On Thursday morning Mother came back from delivering her milk with a dog in the back of the van. One of Mother's customers had asked her if she would like a dog. Mother was not very keen as she already had her own little dog, a mongrel called Judy. The woman told her it belonged to her sister and if Mother didn't have the dog it would be put down. Mother must have taken pity on it because she had gone to Caldmore to collect it. The dog was a lovely short-haired Border Collie about twelve months old. Dad was not too happy when he saw what Mother had come back with, but he couldn't bring himself to see the dog destroyed, so the poor little animal was safe.

When Bill caught site of him and the dog saw Bill they were friends for life. The dog made a right fuss of Bill as if he had known him for years. Bill was very taken with the Collie dog and named him Bob. After that first meeting everywhere Bill went Bob would be right behind him.

Chapter Seventeen

On the Monday following Easter week, Mother took me to Henry Boys and Son's factory in Oxford Street to learn a trade (as she put it). They manufactured articulated trailers and put extra axles onto lorry chassis so they could carry heavier loads. She had arranged for me to be an engineering apprentice and if I didn't like it I could lump it. I got the impression that they were not too keen to have me, but Mother being a friend of the family had talked them into it.

No one interviewed me for the job; I was just told to roll-up at eight o'clock in the morning. When I got there on Tuesday morning I was met by the manager and taken to his office, a shed inside the works. His name was Henry, the eldest of the three brothers who ran the firm and I was to address him as Mr Boys. The normal hours of work would be eight in the morning to twelve thirty then one thirty till six o clock, Monday to Thursday. Eight till five o'clock on Friday and eight till twelve on Saturday morning. But with the 'spiv day' still in operation for the time being the factory worked all day Saturday and had Wednesday afternoon off. I would be expected to attend the technical college on some evenings when the college year started in September. The pay would be at the National Engineering Agreement rates, of seventeen shillings and four pence per week. My first jobs were doing errands and sweeping up, making tea at ten o'clock in the morning and again at three in the afternoon.

The foreman was another brother, his name was Arthur Boys. He was a smashing fellow, everyone got on with him and it was he who made me chief switcher-on. The youngest brother Godfrey ran the drawing and design office in the building down the yard.

The power for all the works machinery was driven by belts which were driven off a shaft that ran the length of the factory. This in turn was driven by a large electric motor at the end of the factory coupled to the shaft by a belt. Arthur showed me how to start it up; you lifted up the lever on the switch gear very slowly and clicked it into the holder. If you lifted the lever too fast it would just cut the motor out, too slow and it wouldn't start at all. My job was to get there just before eight o'clock in the morning and get it going ready for the turners to start work.

There were two turners: Mr Read and Mr Walton and they made the axles for the lorries and trailers. It would be Mr Read who would teach me how to cut a screw thread on a lathe when I did start to use the machinery. He was an interesting old chap who had worked in a factory owned by the French Government during the First World War.

Friday pay-day was the highlight of the week and we stopped work at three o'clock. The last two hours were spent cleaning all the works machinery down and then they were oiled and greased. At ten to five we would all go down to the little office building at the works entrance to collect and sign for our pay. I got seventeen and a penny in my packet – I was stopped two pence hospitals and a penny Red Cross.

I had to hand my pay packet to Mother when I got home. She took ten bob for my board and out of the seven bob left stopped half a crown to buy me a National Savings stamp. That left me with four and seven pence to run wild with and with five Woodbines costing five pence halfpenny I wasn't going to run very wild.

I may have been at work full-time but I was still expected to do a bit round the farm. Working Saturday afternoons got me out of collecting pig food for a while. But as the summer came and we went back to normal hours I would be roped in to help with the collections. We didn't collect from many people now and we usually managed to get it done in a couple of hours. As the year went on, with Dad feeding more meal and potatoes we almost stopped collecting. The only reason we continued was that Dad reckoned the mix of food peelings in the swill made a better feed.

The next disaster was in the early summer. I got home from work for my lunch to find Dad in a bit of a state. He was sat in his armchair coughing and gasping for breath – he looked in a bad way. Dr Davis had been sent for, but he wouldn't be here until he had finished his lunch and cigar. Mother told us that Dad had gone into the field to look at one of the cows, and Bill the bull had charged at him. Dad had made a run for the gate and this was the cause of his coughing and gasping. We all reckoned it was Bill's way of getting back at

Dad for bodging the ring through his nose. Bill had been no trouble before, he had wandered round the yard with the cows during the winter; we would stroke him and he liked his car tickled. The only other time he showed any sign of being a bit nasty was when he would get up to the fence by the path to the park. He would bellow and paw the ground sending up clouds of dust at the people walking their dogs – it was the dogs he took exception to. Most of the dog walkers gave him a wide berth but some took their dogs up to the railings just to get Bill going.

Dad was looking a little better by the time I went back to work but Doctor Davis had not shown up yet. He had recovered enough to be milking the cows when I got home in the evening. He was more upset by Dr Davis who when he came asked Dad, 'what did you run for?' Dad couldn't get over that daft question.

Of course, Mother had to have a punch-up a couple of days later and this was with a street singer. The singer had been coming round the local streets singing for years, he always sang Scottish songs and he wasn't a bad singer. But in Mother's book anyone not working ninety hours a week was a scrounger. So as he was singing his way down Dora Street she had sneaked up to the back of him in the van and blew her horn. The singer took umbrage at what Mother had done and a few heated words were exchanged and they wished one another 'ring of beef' (kiss my arse). It was when Mother drove off that the real crime was committed; the singer had the brass neck to aim a kick at our new van. He missed; a good job or else Mother would have probably run him over with it.

The County Agricultural Show was held in the Arboretum this year but I never got to go due to being at work. Dad and Mom went although Dad didn't show anything. I suppose I could have gone on the weekend but it would have probably cost me all my pocket money to get in.

I think it was at the show that Dad met Reg Noakes who had been Mom and Dad's milkman when they had lived in Palfrey. He had gone back to work delivering milk for the Co-Op after he was demobbed. Reg always started his milk round early and was finished delivering by lunchtime. He now came and did a few odd jobs for Dad on a couple of afternoons a week. I never remember Dad ever paying him but he had eggs and was on the pork and bacon lists and got a share in anything else that was going.

After the bad winter we had a great summer, but as I was at work I missed the best of it although we had some great evenings down the pool and in the park. Watching the tennis players was one of our pleasures; you could see the girl's knickers as they played.

Bill was into fishing now and was off with Jimmy Ash most Sundays fishing pools they were not supposed to. They would fish private pools, Jimmy, Bill and Bill's shadow that daft collie dog Bob, it's a wonder they never got shot for poaching!

In July Dad bought a punt from somewhere, it looked new and we couldn't wait to try it out on the pool. We got on the little truck we collected the pig food with and took it down the water. It was for the fishermen, but bugger the fishermen the Bescot Yacht Club was back! We spent the next few weeks in the punt on the pool at every opportunity. Of course everyone wanted a go in it so Bill and I started charging them three pence a go, once round the pool.

I missed the school holidays and only got one week off from work. I hadn't been there long enough to qualify for the fortnight so I had the last week in July off. The highlight of the week was on Sunday afternoon when a girl in Bill's class at school came and told us her sister was with a sailor in the long grass down by the Bog in the park. Her sister had been writing to the sailor for some time and he was now on leave and had come to visit her. We all climbed onto the railway fence to see what they were up to – some climbed up the railway signal ladders to get a better view. They were going at each other like rabbits and totally oblivious of us all cheering them on. After they had finished the sailor came looking for us but we had vanished by then, a tactical withdrawal I think you would call it. I don't know what he could have done if he had found us, swore us to secrecy perhaps. It was the talk of Gower Street for weeks after.

Granny Mac had gone to visit her sister in Devonshire and our Fanny was to go down there when the school holidays started. When the time came for Fanny to go Mother took her to Brum with her case and a label tied to a button hole of Fanny's coat with her name and destination on it. Fanny also had a letter to give to the station master when she got to London. He would see that she got put on the right train for Exeter where Granny Mac would meet her. We got a postcard a few days later to say Fanny had arrived safe and sound.

All the newspapers were now full of the forthcoming royal wedding of Princess Elizabeth to Prince Philip and of course the women lapped it up. The plumy voiced brigade on the radio, the ones who can talk without moving their lips were telling us all about it and bull about little old dears sending them their margarine rations for their wedding cake and that they would probably have to live in a prefab. Mother and Granny loved it all. Mother's only regret was that she had to deliver the milk on the morning of the wedding so she had to follow the events from door to door as she did her deliveries.

It was now announced by the Government that potatoes would be rationed although bread had been on ration since last year. These were two of the things that had never been rationed during the war. The terrible winter was blamed as the cause of a potato shortage. Dad got a bit worried as he was now relying on them for stock feed. He need not have worried as the quality of stock feed potatoes got better with the rationing.

What happened was the Ministry of Food and Agriculture controlled the amount of potatoes going on the market and once Hydes had supplied their quota they were left with a pile of good spuds. To save them the trouble of camping them, Hydes sold them for stock feed. The man from the Ministry would spray the spuds with blue dye before they left Hydes' yard to stop them being sold on the black market. Half the potatoes didn't get the dye on them so the Sunday morning yard conference gang would help themselves to a few. Sid Perrins used to pick a couple of sacks out for when he went hawking in the afternoon. He paid Dad half a crown a bag for them. Dad was happy he was buying them for twenty-five bob a ton. Although spuds were rationed there never seemed much of a shortage. I think the Government had done it as a precaution just in case there was.

On the first of October 1947 Granddad George died. He was eighty-three. It was a pity he didn't live to see The National Health Service come into being since that would have warmed the cockles of the old bugger's heart. There was a big turn out from the leather industry for his funeral. Through his work he had improved fair play and common decency for leatherworking employees so some employers were probably glad to see the back of him, in their book he was a trouble maker and a malcontent.

As I got home from work for my lunch one day in early December Granny Mac was waiting for me. She took me round to the big fowl pen by the goosegog bushes where Mother was sitting on the fowl perches. You could see she didn't know where she was and she couldn't speak at all. Granny got one side of her and I got the other and we got her back round into the house and sat her in an armchair in Granny's room. No one knew she had been taken ill until someone came to ask why their milk had not been delivered. Granny made Mother comfortable and I stopped at Dr Davies' on my way back to work to ask him to make a call on her. Mother was still in Granny's room when I got home again at about six fifteen. Dr Davis had been and Mother was to go to the hospital. It was quarter to seven when the ambulance came, an old canvas-sided one from the war. Dad was milking so I was sent with Mother in the ambulance to the Manor Hospital. They wouldn't let me in the hospital when they took Mother in. I was told to go home, so I walked back to the farm.

Dad saw John Claridge when he came for the evening milk and gave him a list of Mother's milk customers as he would take over the deliveries.

The farm was a different place without Mother but we all mucked in to try to cover for her absence. Dad visited her every night and Granny would go in the afternoons. Sunday afternoon was the only time children were allowed to visit. Dad took us all up in the van and when we got to the ward the Matron made us stand in line by the door until she told us we could go in and see mother. It was a shock when we got to her bed, she tried to talk to us but we couldn't make out what she was saying. It was hard seeing Mother like this, she had always been so active and even at night after a day's work she would have her book propped up on the table and be knitting as she read it. We were allowed a quarter of an hour before the Matron turfed us out; what we didn't know then was this would be the last time we ever saw her.

In the early hours of Thursday morning the twelfth of December Dad was sent for. He came back home at about seven thirty; he didn't need to tell us what had happened, we knew it was all over for

Mother. According to the death certificate, haemorrhage of the brain was the cause.

Bill was really cut-up over Mother's death, we all were but there were cows to be milked and pigs to be fed. Dad just had to get on with it although we could all see he was in a bit of a state.

I have often thought about it over the years, but I have no recollection of Mother's funeral at all, of who came or anything about it.

I do remember what happened after only too well and I think Dad could have picked a better time to do it. He got Jimmy Harris as a witness and then asked me to go and get Granny Mac from her room. Granny Mac came with her husband's two brothers, the Scots men, who were here for Mother's funeral. Dad told her all the things she had done against him over the years, imagined or otherwise with Mary adding anything he missed. Granny just stood there and never said a word; she would have been wasting her time anyway. She was told she was not welcome here any more and would have to find other accommodation.

It took Granny a couple of days to find somewhere to go and before she went she gave me old Mac's silver watch in the carved wooden box he had always kept it in. I helped Granny get her few sticks of furniture out of her room and we put it in the corner of one of the barns. She was going to her brother Fred's at Sutton for a while until she found herself a permanent place.

On Christmas morning we all mucked in with milking the cows and feeding the pigs and we gave the pigs a good feed to last them until tomorrow. The cows would have to be milked again in the evening.

A miserable Christmas was had by all although Dad cooked us a good dinner. Mother was sorely missed and with no Granny Mac either, it was a sad time.

Dad now convinced me that I should work for him. He reckoned with him not being too good with his chest and just Jacky to help they couldn't manage the farm with just the two of them. I had only started night school in September and would have liked to continue working for Henry Boys but I agreed to work for Dad. He promised to pay me ten shillings a week paid on Friday night when he paid Jacky, but most weeks I had to chase him to get my ten bob out of him. 'Got no change' was his usual excuse.

Chapter Eighteen

The New Year 1948 celebrations were cancelled this year as we felt there was not a lot to celebrate.

The papers kept telling us things were getting better. The only improvement we could see was that from February you could buy clothes without coupons but that was if you could find some to buy. A man had opened a stall on Lichfield Market selling American army surplus clothes and boots and Dad used to keep us well togged up with these; most of the country's manual workers wore old army wear. The old great coats were lovely in the cold weather and both Bill and I had one. Our Fanny was a bit more fashion conscious but Granny had taught her how to knock up a skirt or blouse for herself on the sewing machine from a bit of old parachute nylon, so she was alright.

With my new wealth I was able to join some of my friends on their Saturday night trips to the pictures. When I could get my ten bob out of Dad by Saturday, that is. We would scrub ourselves up, make sure we had a clean shirt and borrow one of Dad's ties; well, we wanted to look like the gentlemen we thought we were. On one Saturday I had no hair cream so I used a bit of pork dripping instead to stick my hair down. Bill told everyone I had dripping on my hair. I never lived it down, even sixty years later he still calls me Mickey Dripping. We would go down to Walsall on the top deck of a Walsall Corporation bus and join the queue for the film and go in the one and nine pennies. Men of our means couldn't be seen in the ten penny seats, could we? To round the night off on our way home we would call at Hicklings off licence on the Darlaston Road and splash out on a couple of bottles of family ale. These were shared by four or five of us and drank in the little passage that ran up to Narrow Lane. We always took the bottles back and got the two pence off them before we went home. Boy, this was really living!

Working for Dad meant I had swapped an eight hour a day job for a twenty-four hours a day one. The plus side was that I got out in the van with Jacky more and we would be off most mornings after milking and feeding the pigs. Our first trip on Tuesday was to Highgate Brewery for the grains, the spent malt after it had been mashed. These were sold by the bushel and we measured them as four shovels to the bushel onto the van. The best part of this trip was the free beer. Mr White who supervised the grain sales had a large enamel jug and when anyone came for the grains he would fill it with beer for them. I wasn't supposed to be having any but Jacky always gave me a drop.

Fetching the waste out of the Co-Op bakery was another good trip since you got some new bread. We now had the contract to clear the waste out of Cannock bakery as well. They were not as generous as Walsall; we got no new bread from them. The Bakery trips were great in the cold weather as it was always nice and warm in there so if it was a cold day we took our time getting the old flour and bread out.

Meal and dairy nuts now had to be fetched from the railway goods yard in Aldridge. Stanley's in Bridge Street had closed; I think old Stanley had died. Dad was now having his feed from Silcocks and they had a little depot in the goods shed at Aldridge railway station. The drive there was the best bit of this trip; we would go through Walsall and on to the Melish Road. This road had a dual carriage way and no speed limit so Jacky would drive flat out down it. He would get the van doing over sixty miles an hour but try as he might he could never reach sixty-five. However it was an exiting ride.

The rat catcher had been working there one day when we went for dairy nuts, he lived in Queen Street and we offered him a lift back to Walsall. I had to climb on top of the diary nuts in the back of the van with the catchers three dog's; two terriers, a lurcher, and a box of ferrets.

It wasn't long before we were wishing we had not offered the lift back to Walsall as he stunk the van out. God did he smell and when Jacky opened the window, with me being in the back of the van, I got the full benefit of him. We had some strong odours on the farm at times; but he beat anything we had ever smelt. It was a great relief when we got into Walsall and dropped him off by the Bradford Street Bus Station – never again.

When we got back to the yard we found Dad hanging on a pigsty door gasping for breath. He had been cleaning out Fred the old large white boar. Fred had taken exception to Dad and had tried to tusk him, Dad had managed to get out of the sty but Fred had ripped his trousers. This little episode proved to be the end of Fred; he was getting on a bit anyway. He had only lasted so long because he fathered big litters and had been reliable.

A new boar was now needed and Dad could have got one off Percy Haines but he wanted one that had a proven record. He finally found one at a farm that was closing down at Bradley. Wolverhampton Council was building houses on his farm so he had to sell up. Arrangements were made to go and collect the pig with the van but the boar was too big to have loose in the motor. Harry Bagnal, who was now retired and not bad at a bit of carpentry, was fetched by Dad to cut a pig crate down so we could get it in the van. He was coming in the summer to do some whitewashing anyway. Harry cut six inches off the top of a crate and took the wheels off so we could just get it in the van. The crate was just high enough to get the pig in and it took four of us to fetch him. Dad was driving, Reg Noakes was in the passenger seat and me and Jacky in the back, one each side of the crate. We called the new boar Bobtail because his tail had been bitten off. But he proved to be a good boar; he was nice and long and fathered big litters.

Old Fred was sold to one of Jeff Slater's mates who had bought most of Dad's old sows in the last couple of years. He was turning them into bacon and selling it on the black market to some hotel in Brum. I bet old Fred would be a bit tough to chew though.

Ken Taylor had now got married to girl called Eileen from down south and she had a little boy named Graham. Like everyone else who got wed these days it was finding somewhere to live that was the problem. The war had ended three years ago but houses were in very short supply and lots of families where still squatting in old army camps. So, Dad told Aunty Sarah, Ken's mother, Eileen and her son Graham could come and live with us. Bill and I got on well with them but our Fanny was a bit offish. Since Mother had died she was going to be Queen Bee, wasn't she.

Dad still paid a woman from the top of Gower Street to come and do a bit of cleaning on two mornings a week but Eileen did most of the cooking and the food was better with her doing it. Things went well for about three months until one afternoon Jacky and I were coming down Gower Street in the van and met Eileen and Graham going to the bus stop. Eileen had been crying and she had her cases with her. She wouldn't tell us what had gone off; only that she was going to Auntie Sarah's. We never did find out what had gone on that afternoon.

Jacky was now courting; it had started as pen friends. Jacky had found the address in a box of milk filters some time ago and started writing to her. It was now getting more serious with Jacky going to Chesterfield to visit her some weekends 'plighting his troth' Harry Bagnal called it.

One Monday morning Granny Mac came, she must have seen Dad go off to Lichfield Market. She had a man with a pony and cart with her. The man had come to buy her few sticks of furniture out of the barn. They were there for some time haggling over the furniture and I think she ended up with about seven pounds ten shilling. Granny seemed happy with it and I helped load it on the cart. She asked me how I liked the cake she sent me for my birthday – but what cake? I hadn't seen one. Dad usually collected the post so he must have had it and probably threw it on the boiler.

Granny told me she was now lodging with a widow who lived in the Butts and gave me her address so I could visit her. She was sorry I never got my cake, so was I, but she gave me five bob out of the furniture money before she went. Bill and Mary were at school so they didn't see Granny.

Dad never said anything about Granny coming for her stuff although he must have noticed it had gone; I never mentioned the missing cake to Dad since I thought it best to say nothing.

My main interest on the farm was the pigs; I was never very keen on the cows. I did a bit of milking sometimes but only when I couldn't get out of doing it, like when Dad was a bit rough with his chest. He had been better this year, not coughing so much and he said he felt a lot better than he had for years. He now convinced himself that he had improved since Mother's death and that was because Mother and Granny had been poisoning him. However, he had been cutting down on the self cure he was taking and that was probably one of the reasons why he felt a lot better. Dad was even more convinced that Granny and Mother were trying to see him off when he found some correspondence hidden in a cupboard. It seems that Mother had been looking at buying a couple of houses in Slaney Road as an investment. That made Dad's day when he found the papers. In his book it was proof of their plans to get rid of him; well that's what he was telling everyone.

A couple of pigs had been butchered for Easter last year and with the help of Jeff Slater a couple more were killed this Easter. Meat was still rationed and hard to get hold of so there was always a ready market for pork. It was cash in pocket, no paperwork or questions asked. Of course you had to be careful who you sold it to but there was always a good supply of black market buyers ready to help you out.

I only got to go to Lichfield Market with Dad on the odd occasion now. The first time this year was just before the Easter holiday weekend and was for me to bid for a couple of orphan lambs while Dad was at the pig pens. I was sent to the sheep pens with the strict instruction not to bid above seven and six pence each for them. In the event I got them for four and a tanner each. We would have to bottle feed them for a few weeks as usual but we had plenty of milk. We all looked forward to our bit of lamb in the autumn now.

Chapter Nineteen

I got a present for my fifteenth birthday in 1948. It was a month late and I wasn't expecting anything and I didn't get a card off anyone. Granny very likely sent me one but with Dad collecting the mail he would probably have burnt it with the cake.

I got a little shotgun off Dad; it was from one of young Bill Taylor's in-laws. Bill and his brother Doug had married two sisters who had lived in Ward Street and their father had a nine millimetre shotgun he wanted to sell. Dad and I went down there after tea one evening to have a look at it. The man wanted fifteen bob but Dad knocked him down to twelve and a tanner, so we bought it. It was a nice little gun made in Belgium and very simple to load. There were a couple of dozen cartridges with it and what we didn't know at the time was that we would have trouble getting any more. I was happy with it until I came to buy some more ammunition for it. None of the sporting shops in Walsall sold cartridges of that bore. They only stocked the popular sizes like twelve, sixteen and four-ten bores. The only place we could get them was from the gun shops in Steel House Lane in Brum. Dad bought a box of fifty when he went to Brum once, but I think that was the only box we ever had.

Dad had ten cows milking now and had not kept any calves for some time. He would butcher one for veal occasionally and have the hide made into the famous travel bags. They were always in demand and fetched more than the calf was worth. It was always a bull calf he killed, the heifer calves he would take into Lichfield Market. If he wanted to replace a cow these days he would buy one which was due to calf from the market. The bull had been tied up with the cows in the shed all winter and was no trouble even when he was let loose in the yard with the cows for a bit of exercise.

It was now time to turn the cows out to graze and the bull with them. I could see Dad was a bit worried about it as there were stories of accidents with Friesian bulls in the *Farmer and Stockbreeder* every week. Bill got turned out with the cows but was not allowed to come in at milking time. He was alright when he was with the cows but when they were not there that was when he got a bit nasty. The barn by the field had a door which opened on to it and Dad's plan was to entice Bill into the barn before he let the cows in. There was another door opposite the field door that opened into the yard. The drill was this: wait until the cows came to the field gate at milking time and then open the barn door into the field. Bill would then be enticed into the barn and then we would bolt through the other door into the yard, nip round into the field and shut the barn door. A hand full of dairy nuts had been what Dad had used to get the bull into the barn and after a couple of times Bill would go in himself when you opened the door as long as you left him a few nuts. When the cows returned to the field after milking you opened the barn door then climbed into the loft above it until Bill had gone off with the cows. His downfall was to come later in the year. The Ministry of Agriculture had opened a place near Sutton Coldfield to do artificial insemination of dairy cattle. It had been set up as part of the Government's plan to improve the quality of dairy cattle. They kept bulls from the country's best milking herds there. At twenty-five bob a time to serve a cow it wasn't worth keeping a bull so poor old Bill had to go. He went to Lichfield Market and was bought by another farmer to serve his cows. There were a lot of farmers who didn't like the idea of artificial insemination; their view was the Government would be getting rid of men next.

As the weather got better, a lot of my evenings after tea were spent down the pool or in the park. Sunday afternoons was about the only time I had off in the daytime these days. If I could manage to sneak off for a couple of hours on Saturday I would go to the baths. One of my treats was to have a swim, and still is. Floating on my back in the brine bath, I'm in another world.

With the Bescot yacht club being back in business and only the punt to sail for the whole membership, I was first to grab it. I jumped in it one night when Bill wanted it. He found a length of old railway fence and tried to pull me back with it. There was a nail in the end of it that caught on Bill's wrist and cut it. There was blood everywhere and it was lucky Masso Bird was by the pool since he was a member of the St John Ambulance Brigade. He put a band round Bill's arm and slowed the blood flow. We took Bill home and Dad drove him to the General hospital out-patients department. The nail had poked a hole in Bill's wrist but not cut it so he didn't get any stitches, they just put a pad and a large plaster on it. After a week Bill was as good as new again and ready for the fishing season to start.

When it did in June, Bill and Jimmy Ash were off on their Sunday fishing trips again. I never got very keen. I used to do some fishing with a long cane I used for a rod that I got from Jones's corn and seed shop in the Pleck.

Another vessel was acquired for the yacht club from an Army surplus shop in Bilston. A one-man dingy it was supposed to be, but we didn't let that stop us from getting two or three of us in it. I went and fetched it one Saturday afternoon with a gang of friends on our bikes. Fifty bob it cost and Dad gave me the money to buy it with.

We were down by the pool fishing one evening when there was a deep roaring noise. The water at the far end of the pool seemed to rise up several feet and a wave of water came rushing down the pool. As the pool calmed down some dead fish came floating up. Finny Humphries, one of the keen fishermen who was there reckoned it was an unexploded bomb. It must have been dropped when the railway line near James Bridge was bombed and had just decided to explode. There could have been other bombs in the pool but that didn't stop us swimming and paddling in it.

Once I had got used to working for Dad I found more time to do my own things. You were not governed by the clock like in a factory. Cows were milked before feeding the pigs in the morning but in the evening it was the other way round, pigs fed first. There was no exact time to do it. The hours of daylight dictated when things could be done, so earlier in the summer and later in the winter. Another thing was that call-up for the forces had been started again, National Service they were calling it. If you worked in agriculture you were exempt and the only other way to get out of it was to go down the pit and be a coal miner.

I even did a bit of cooking; you had to these days if you wanted to eat. Dad or Fanny usually did it but Dad mainly and his best dish was grey peas and bacon, we all liked that. A tray of toffee was another of his treats but he only made that when he could swap some bacon for a bag of sugar from someone. When he could get his hands on a bit of beef he would have a jar of stew on the hob.

Meat was still rationed and we were registered at Collins for ours and one of us would collect it on a Saturday. If it was beef we would be getting stew next week. Any other meat was used for our Sunday lunch, always cooked by Dad and whatever we had he always did Yorkshire pudding with it. If the week's beef was our ration we would have our home-cured bacon for Sunday lunch. The grocery items that were still on ration Dad bought from Coopers Grocers, who had their shop in Dickinson Drive. Mother had changed from Parkers to them when they started to buy their milk off us. These were always fetched on Friday afternoon and Dad would bring me twenty cigarettes with them most weeks. Meal times had gone out of the window since Mother's death except for Sunday lunch. Meals were on a help yourself when you wanted it basis. Still we did alright and none of us went hungry.

In the summer Dad found himself a new hobby; he placed a dustbin upside down against the fence that separated the farm from the old tip. The path to the park ran alongside this fence and about seven o'clock every night if the weather was fine he would go and stand on the dustbin. He was chatting up the women walking their dogs to the park. It wasn't long before he was taking a young war widow who lived in Kingsley Street out for a drink. She must have been twenty years younger than Dad but that didn't put him off. She wasn't the only one he was taking for a quiet drink; the woman who issued the ticket for us to get the grains at Highgate Brewery was another. Jacky and I had wondered why he suddenly decided to fetch the brewery grains himself. We now knew why.

He took one or two out over the next few months. He was shampooing his hair three times a week now and doing himself up like a prize terrier before he went out. A gentleman farmer or so he thought he was, still it kept him happy. While he was occupied taking his lady friends for a drink, I could go up the Butts and see Granny Mac. If any questions were asked as to where I had been, I told them down the Arboretum.

In the late summer we started to get all the jobs on Saturday done by one o'clock. This gave us about three hours off before feeding pigs and milking cows. Dad usually had visitors anyway – Sid Lewis would come yapping; Dad's brother George was another regular

126

when Walsall football team were playing at home, he would call after the match. It was on one of these afternoons that my little car went missing, A Schuco clockwork car with three forward gears and a reverse gear and you could turn the front wheels of the car with the steering wheel. Jacky had given it to me shortly after he started working at the farm. I had always kept it in the cupboard where Dad put all his paperwork and I hadn't missed it until I came to show it to someone weeks later. That was when our Fanny told me with some glee Dad had given it to Sid Lewis for his son to play with.

The pear harvest went mainly to rot this year. Bill tried to sell a few but with oranges and some foreign fruit now back in the shops no one wanted hard pears. The apples we put on the floor of an empty bedroom individually wrapped in paper, and they lasted well into the spring. With us now getting regular loads of potatoes off Hydes we didn't need to save any for the winter.

Dad now decided to tog Bill and me up with some new clothes before the winter came. Both of us were getting a bit tired of running around in old army gear. He got his sister Sarah to sort Fanny out with her new rig-out. We were taken to a shop in Caldmore, the proprietor being a friend of Dad's brother Albert. A pair of corduroy trousers and a shirt was bought for each of us. They were a size too large, the idea being that we would grow into them.

Our next trip was to Wolverhampton. Dad had seen an advert in the *Express and Star* about a shop in the Arcade there selling leather bomber jackets. We were taken over there one afternoon and Bill had to have time off from school to go. Jackets in brown leather were bought for all of us and even Dad had one. I think the motive for smartening us up was that Dad had taken to going to the cinema. Thursday night was the usual time since the queue to get in would be shorter. Most people got paid on Friday and by Thursday of the next week had spent it all and couldn't afford to go to the cinema. Dad had always taken us with him when he went and I don't think he wanted to be seen standing in the queue with what looked like a couple of refugees.

In the autumn we made a work bench in the room at the end of the barn to do a bit of woodwork on. This place had a little stove in the corner as it had always been our gang's hut. In the evenings after tea when we had finished listening to *Dick Barton Special Agent* on the radio we planned to do a bit of carpentry. We couldn't start any earlier because we had to wait until after the cows had been milked so we could borrow the lamps. They were pressure lamps and you had to pump them up and the gas from the pressurised paraffin lit the mantel in them. Dad had bought them from Lichfield Market and they gave a much better light than the old hurricane lamps with wicks in.

Sid Perrins supplied most of our wood which were old fruit boxes. Most of them were soft wood and easy to cut. Dolls House furniture was one of the things we made and also some models of warships off plans we got from the hobby shop. We did sell a few bits of it through Seagraves shop in Kingsley Street. They put them in their shop window and take them out again after a week if they had not sold. We didn't sell many and we only got a few coppers for them if they did sell. Seagraves kept half the money for selling them; still it was better than nothing.

It was during one of our woodworking evenings I got my finger and thumb bruised. One of our friends opened the door and threw a firework in while we were at the bench. It was a banger and landed in the top of one of Bill's wellingtons. I grabbed it and just as I was going to throw it back it exploded. The sides of my thumb and forefinger of my right hand turned blue and they were a bit sore for a few days. Having bruised fingers didn't get me out of doing jobs on the farm; Dads view was if you can't use your right hand use your left.

Things were back to normal this Christmas, well almost. Dad and Jeff slaughtered more pigs and we did the pork and chicken deliveries to the pig food savers as usual. The only difference this year was a lot of the people who had ordered fowl wanted them dressed. People were getting too posh to pluck and draw their own; 'oven-ready' was the order of the day. Bill took on the job of doing them and charged two bob each for his trouble.

A leg of pork was kept for our Christmas dinner and the rest of the meat sold. With meat still strictly rationed and the festive season here, plenty of spare cash was made.

Dad and Fanny cooked our dinner on Christmas day and it was a good feed but not the same with Mom and Granny gone. I think we all missed them more than we had last year, I know Bill and I did.

Chapter Twenty

Over the Christmas and New Year, Dad had been spending his Saturday nights with his brother George and his wife Maud, drinking in the Fullbrook Pub. His eldest sister Dora was also a regular visitor for her glass of bitter, (a bit genteel was Aunty Dora, she couldn't be seen swigging pints.) After the pub closed it had always been their practice to take some beer home with them and have a bit of a party. There were a few of their friends in the smoke room who would join them and Dad was usually one of them. It would one or two o'clock in the morning before he came home. This didn't bother Bill or me but our Fanny made out she was very concerned. Fanny set out to go and find Dad on a couple of occasions and she would dress herself up before she set out. Bill and I soon realized it was not Dad's welfare she was concerned about but the fact she was missing the party. However, her walk all up to George and Maud's house in Tame Street in the middle of the night did her no good at all. As soon as she got there Dad brought her straight back home.

Most Saturday night's Bill and I along with some of our friends would go to Wolverhampton to the Roller Drome. After all the milking and pig feeding was done we would posh ourselves up in our new leather jackets and meet our friends at the bus stop, catch the through bus from the top of Gower Street to Wolverhampton and walk up to the Roller Drome. The cost of entry ticket also included the hire of the roller skates. We had some great evenings and a few tumbles in there but it was all part of the fun. I think it had been an old factory before it was a skating rink. That's probably why it was always very dusty in there. They closed at ten o'clock but we had to leave before then as the last bus back to Walsall was at ten.

The ride back home through Bilston and Darlaston was usually very entertaining. Ten o'clock was pub closing time and you got a few of the boozing gang on the bus and most of them were comedians or singers but it was all in good fun. I never remember any fighting or violence breaking out although the bus conductor had his work cut out keeping a bit of order.

The pool froze thick enough for us to skate on but only for a couple of days in January. Bill and I were down on it one of the evenings having a slide when two chaps came to do a bit of duck shooting. I had my little nine millimetre shot gun with me for the same reason. One of the chaps had a sixteen-bore double barrel shotgun and the other a Lincoln Jeffries air rifle like the one Dad had bought for Bill and me. The one with the Lincoln Jeffries liked my little shotgun and offered to swap me his air rifle for it. I could see it was worth a lot more than my gun and with the cartridges so hard to get I agreed. Dad had loaned our Lincoln Jeffries rifle to Jack Evans last September to do a bit of ratting and we hadn't seen it since. Everyone reckoned I had a good deal and Dad decided we should have it refurbished. Mr Marsden who was the traveller for Silcocks, came to get our order for meal and dairy nuts a few days later. He had a brother who was a gunsmith and said he would refurbish the air rifle for us. He took it with him and when it came back a fortnight later it was as new, they had made a great job of it. Of course a week later Jack Evans rolled up with our old one so Bill and I now had one each.

Early in the New Year the Council started to build houses on the old tip. They had levelled it all off last autumn. Most of the oak and elm trees had been chopped down then but they had left the silver beech trees on the corner of the lane for the time being. They were old magnificent trees that shone bright in the sun, but that didn't save them, they had to come down later just to gain another foot of building land.

Farming was on the up these days and we still had ten milking cows but our main product now was producing bacon pigs. The barn by the field was turned into a large sty to hold about thirty. A couple of the old farrowing pens were knocked into one. Dad only kept two or three sows to fiddle the pig count as there were still checks by the Ministry on pig numbers, what was bred against what were sent for slaughter. Buying in store pigs was now the order of the day, mainly from Lichfield Market. Dad went there most Mondays and even if he wasn't buying it was a social gathering with his cronies. When Dad was buying he would take me with him to learn how to bid. The practice I had bidding in the fowl and pets shed didn't count up here where you were playing with the big boys. I was pretty good at picking out a good pig myself but with Dad's help I would get it down to a fine art. We bought mainly large white crosses at six to eight weeks old as they were always 'good doers'.

When bidding, you needed to know when to go in and when to drop out. Sometimes I would bid for some myself with Dad's tuition; he stood behind me telling me when to bid and when to pull out. Well he wasn't going to let me go wild with his money was he? I was only a learner.

One buying trip always sticks out in my memory and it was not to Lichfield market. It was on a January morning and to Rodbaston Agricultural College at Penkridge. The reason I remember it so well is that I never felt as cold in my life as I did that morning. The college was holding an auction of breeding pigs from their herd of large whites and Dad was looking to buy a young boar. The sale was held in a Dutch barn and I'm sure it was ten degrees colder in there that it was outside. I thought I would never get warm again and there was nowhere to get a hot drink. We didn't buy since the prices were a bit too rich for Dad to swallow and the drive home in the van didn't help me to get warm as it was before the days of heaters in motors. I spent the first hour at home hugging the pig food boiler; it took me all day to get warm again.

The Agricultural College sale was the only other sale we did; Lichfield was our main market, buying in and feeding pigs up to between ten and twelve score then sending them for slaughter. Most went to Millward & Burrell's slaughterhouse in West Bromwich and Jeff Slater worked there so he could keep an eye on the pigs Dad sent in. Even so, there were a couple of times Dad reckoned the dead weights he got back were not what he sent in. He got a bit paranoid at times like his brother Albert; he thought everyone was out to do him. As usual our Harry was a man with a plan. Using a piece of leather we used to sole our boots with and some brads, he knocked the brads through the leather to spell 'Power' and then nailed the strip of leather with the brads sticking up onto a block of wood. The next time pigs were sent for slaughter Dad wiped it with black lead, placed it on the pig's back and hit it with a mallet. Jeff reported back that after the pigs had been scrapped and dressed you could still see 'Power' tattooed on them. It was only skin deep so we got no complaints about it and everyone was happy and making money.

Farming was now starting to pay off and it's a pity Mother didn't live long enough to see it.

It was now decided we needed a new steam boiler as our old boiler had been leaking for years. The search was on for a good second-hand one but it took a while to find it. We finally found one for sale at The Midland Counties Dairy at Wolverhampton, they were modernizing and getting rid of their old coal-fired boilers. It was in very good condition and had been well looked after so Dad bought it. Jacky and I got the old boiler out and it didn't take us long; we just disconnected it, tipped it over and rolled it down the pig field out of the way. Mr Reynolds one of Dad's drinking pals came and put the new boiler in and advised that it would be better lagged or 'monkey mucked' as he called it. This was done by one of Jeff Slater's relations, Horace Slater who was the boiler man at Prices Mill. After he had finished the lagging Dad got him to fit another pipe to the steam system which was run under the yard to the bathroom. The pipe was then put through the wall and into the bath to warm the water for us to have a bath. This saved us the trouble of having to light the copper every time we wanted a bath but the problem was that you could only have a bath when the boiler was on to cook the pig food.

There were not so many cart horses turned out for a rest this year since a lot of the coal yards were now getting lorries. Heavy draft horses were not wanted anymore and lorries were quicker. Boot and Lancaster's still turned a couple out in our field along with Sid Perrins and old Wallwoods' mare. The only other carthorse that came these days was Fred Walters' big horse Captain who drew Fred's old tipcart. He was a lovely big chestnut horse with four white socks and a white blaze and must have been over eighteen hands. He was a sight to behold on May Day when Fred would plait his mane and tail with red, white and blue ribbons. The carters had always done their horses up for May Day but since the war it was starting to die out. Captain belonged to Fred who did a bit of hauling mainly for the foundries along the Pleck Road. They would come occasionally when Fred had the order for a load of muck for the allotments. It was always a bit of a laugh when they fetched a load as Fred would back the cart up to the muckheap and every fork of muck he threw on the cart Fred would call 'wow cap' although the horse had never moved. This 'wow capping' went on all the while he was loading the cart, it's a wonder it didn't get on the horse's wick. Harry Titley still came to exercise Herbert Field's hackney horses when the weather was good but Dawson had given up on his race horses by now.

Our next excitement came on Easter Saturday. Dad and Jeff had killed some pigs for the black market. It was all cash in hand and no receipts or questions asked. His sister Sarah had a couple to sell in her butcher's shop at Shelfield but only to her special customers. It was about ten o'clock on the Saturday morning when a chap came flying into our yard on his bike, all hot and bothered. The police had raided Aunty Sarah's shop and she still had some of our pork. Aunt Sarah had sold a joint to one of her customers who had gone and told her sister who had gone to the shop and asked for a joint. Sarah told her she had none, the woman was not even rationed with her. The woman then went and blew the whistle on Aunty selling black-market meat and her shop was raided by the Police and a Ministry official.

Dad still had some pork hanging in the cellar and we had to move it quick but he had kept some new clean dustbins for such an emergency. The next half hour was all go as we loaded the pork into the bins and put it in the van. Jacky and I were then sent to his brother George to hide it in their coal house. It got Aunty Maud in a bit of a tizzy but she calmed down after a couple of fags. Jacky and I had got back to our yard before the Police came roaring up the drive in their old Rover followed by the man from the Ministry. They got Dad in the house for questioning while a sergeant and a couple of constables searched the house and the barns. They found nothing as all the evidence had been shifted; Dad had even put his knives in the dustbins we took to Uncle George's. After checking the cow shed and the entire pig sties they went, but it's a good job they never dug the muckheap over.

I helped Dad fetch the pork back after dark and it was all cut into joints as soon as we got it home. Bill and I did late night deliveries; well they wanted it for their Easter Sunday lunch. No more was ever heard about it, and anyway Dad reckoned that they wouldn't push it

as there were one or two members of The Walsall Borough
Constabulary who had been on the pork list for years!

Chapter Twenty-One

The Easter week turned out to be very eventful this year; not only did Bill and Fanny leave school but Jacky Shut got married as well. Jacky had booked the Easter week off and had gone up to Chesterfield to wed the woman whose address he found in the box of milk filters. His parents were the only folks from Walsall to attend. I never remember any of us being invited; if we were Dad never told us.

After the Bank Holiday weekend was over Dad got us kids together to sort out what we were all going to do. We were not asked for our opinions as it was obvious Dad had already decided. Bill would be the cowman as he was the best at milking; I would continue doing mainly the pigs. Fanny, (everyone called her Fanny these days, even Dad) would look after the house. We would all get the same pay of a pound each a week, when we could get it out of him! I didn't get any extra for being older; still it was double the ten bob I had been getting.

The woman who did a bit of cleaning for us still came on a couple of days each week. Jacky was not as lucky as he was now entitled to the married man's pay rate. The tripe 'supper money' he had been paid before, on the excuse the job was keeping him from being called up, wouldn't wash anymore. On the Saturday morning after Easter week, Jacky and his new wife came back to Walsall to live with his mother. Dad put on his best suit and went up to see Jacky to give him the sack on the grounds he couldn't afford to pay the married man's rate. I don't suppose Jacky was very happy about it but what could he do. Any time later when Dad got togged up in his suit we would say to one another, mind your step – be careful he's got his sacking suit on! Later we heard from Harry Titley, Jackie's cousin, that sacking Jacky had done him a favour; he had now got a farming job with a cottage to live in as part of the job.

One day as Bill was getting the cows in for milking he found a young wood pigeon on the ground. It had fallen out of one of the elm trees in the meadow where the wood pigeons nested every year. Bill put it in an old rabbit hutch that was propped against the wall of the dairy to keep it away from the cats. He fed it two or three times a day until it was fully feathered and could fly up onto the dairy roof. It soon flew away and we thought that was the last we would see of it, but just before it got dark it came back and roosted in the hutch. Bill fed it some wheat and it had gone again when we got up next morning. It came back again at dusk to roost but was gone at first light the following day and we never saw it again. There were no feathers in the hutch so we didn't think the cats had taken it.

Rearing the wood pigeon had both Bill and I interested in pigeons, we had to have some. Our woodwork bench in the barn was pulled down and we divided the room in half with wire netting. Pigeons were acquired from anywhere we could get them and we had a mixture of tumbler tipplers and racing pigeons. When we first had them we couldn't let them out for a fly around, if we did they would fly back home. The answer to this problem was cutting some of their flight feathers off one of their wings. You could then let them out for a run around on the yard and by the time their feathers had grown again they would be used to their new home. Even after doing this some of them would still go back to where they had come from and we would usually have trouble getting them back again as the person you had bought it off would deny it had returned. After about a month we had probably ten or so broken in and used to their surroundings so they didn't fly off.

Alfie Parker was taking some of his young racing pigeons up to West Bromwich old church to start their training flight one Saturday morning. Bill and I sent a couple of our birds with them and they came back home alright so we were over the moon!

It was on the following Sunday lunchtime we got into trouble. Bill and I had our pigeons out and they were all perched on the barn roof and we were trying to get them down to put them back in the pen. Fanny had come out of the house and told us our dinner was ready and on the table. We stood there shaking our tins of corn and calling the pigeons down but they wouldn't budge. Dad was the next one to come and tell us to get in the house for our lunch, but we still stood there shaking our tins. A couple of minutes later Dad came out with his twelve bore shotgun and let the pigeons on the roof have a barrel. Two of the birds came down right away dead, one of them my favourite pigeon, a blue badge, the rest flew off.

Dad never liked us keeping pigeons anyway, he always referred to them as them 'bloody wofflers' but I think he had got his arse in his hand this lunch time over something else.

He had been sparking up a young widow who lived in Bescot Street since Christmas and she had been for Sunday lunch with us on a couple of occasions. Our Harry was togged up in his sacking suit for lunch so I think she should have come today. She never turned up, so not only was it the end of our pigeon flying but the end of a beautiful romance as well.

Building was going on all around us and now they had started to build on the old allotments next to our top field. There were also large structures appearing on the skyline – the cooling towers for the new power station being built at Reedswood. They were massive and we had never seen anything that large before. We did alright off the people who were building on the old allotments since every evening they would give any cement left over when they finished work. We would go and fetch it in the van and lay it on the yard by the muckheap so it made the yard a lot tidier and the ground firmer for Hyde's lorry to park when they fetched the muck.

Dad thought he had heard the last of the Easter pork affair but he was wrong. He got a visit by a couple of the Bowler hat brigade from the Ministry of Agriculture offices in Stafford. They were here to view his pig breeding records, such as they were. Or as Dad succinctly put it, wanting to know 'Meg's arse and the road to it'. Our father was never one for paperwork so they were never going to learn much from it. His milking records were only right because John Claridge kept them up to date for him. However they spent all morning studying the old receipt book he used to record the pig litters in and questioned Dad for half the morning. They found nothing to charge him with, well nothing they could prove and cleared off back to Stafford shaking their heads. I don't think they had ever seen book-keeping like it before.

It was only about a week later when he was in trouble again. Under the National Insurance Act he should have registered himself as self employed and us three kids as his employees. Dad was summoned to the department of National Insurance to their offices at the old Wigmore Schools at West Bromwich to explain why he hadn't bothered to register. He must have told them a good tale as it all got sorted out at the Walsall office; their headquarters was in an old Chapel in Bridge Street. Dad didn't like having to pay National Insurance stamps but he had to lump it, a lot of his farming cronies had tried to dodge paying the insurance stamps as well but the Department of Employment was now starting to round them up.

Things on the farm were now running like clockwork with Bill and me and we also had Reg most afternoons to help. Harry Bagnall only came in the spring and summer to gas tar and repair the roofs and do the whitewashing. Dad would go and fetch old Harry in the mornings after milking and take him home at teatime. He always thought a lot of Harry as he had helped Father a lot when he first started farming. Jacky was missed for driving the van and Dad was our main driver now although Reg would take us to collect pig food some afternoons as he had a driving licence too. Some days we would go out to fetch the waste from the Co-Op bakery later in the morning. This was when Dad was having a bet on the horses. Howard the bookie's runner had moved from Gower Street and was now standing on the Goscote crossroads between twelve and one o'clock midday. Going out later allowed Dad to clear the Co-Op waste then call round and hand in his bet all in one trip. Why he couldn't have had a bet with old Parlow who stood by the Police box at the Brown Lion instead of going all the way to Goscote, nobody could work out.

In the main things were going well and Fanny was our only problem. Now she had been appointed house keeper you would have thought she was Lady Muck and she had become a right pain. She had sold most of Mother's clothes to Mrs Plant and kept the money for herself. Dad must have known what she was doing but never said anything to her about it.

Bill didn't do much fishing this season; he was kept busy like me. I don't remember him having a Sunday fishing trip with Jimmy Ash at all. Well he had two milking sessions to do on Sundays, morning and again in the evenings. He still enjoyed a bit of fishing and would be down the pool for a couple of hours some nights. We were both down there one evening in the early summer, Bill fishing and me on the punt when someone fishing off the railway bank caught a pike. It caused a right commotion as it was probably the biggest fish any of us had ever seen and as far as anybody knew there were no pike in the pool. Jimmy Ash still had his boiler suit on from work with his measuring tape in the pocket so the fish was measured on the spot. Two foot six and a half inches long but we never found out what the weight of it was. Word soon got round a large pike had been caught and for the next couple of weeks everyone was down there pike fishing.

Things calmed down after a while until early one morning when the Police came knocking on our door. Passengers on the Walsall to Wolverhampton train had reported a body floating in our pool. The two constables went down the field to have a look but soon came back and used their car radio to call for help. After a while a van came with a Sergeant and a Constable wearing overalls. They drove the van down to the pool and the Constable put on a pair of waders and went in and pulled the body out of the water. We could all see who it was even before the body was out of the pool; it was Finny Humphries the fisherman. The Sergeant and Constable laid Finny out in the back of the van, covered him up and drove off. There was a report in *The Walsall Observer* about it and an inquest, the verdict was suicide. It was all a bit sad as he had no family anybody could trace and had lodged with a family who lived in Dora Street since the end of the First World War.

The Royal Agricultural Show was to be held at Shrewsbury this year and Dad decided we should have a day out there. On the great day the cows had been milked and pigs fed and we were on our way by eight thirty; Father driving, with Bill and I in the back of the van and one of Harry Bagnal's relations, Bill Stiles, in the passenger seat.

We got to the showground by the River Severn at about ten thirty. Dad and Bill Stiles spent most of the day going round the trade stalls and yapping at the pig lines. Bill and I had a quick look around then found us a good seat by the show ring. It was heavy horse day and there were some magnificent horses being shown all done up in their ribbons, coats gleaming in the sun. In the afternoon it was the teams of horses to be judged; there were three classes: pairs, and four in hand and six in hand. I think most of the sixes in hand belonged to timber merchants. Over the years these horses and their wagons have been my abiding memory of this day-out I have never seen anything like it since that day. We had to leave the show at four o'clock to get home and feed the pigs and do the milking. The cows were milked first tonight to make sure the milk would be ready for John Claridge to collect at seven thirty.

Chapter Twenty-Two

Dad and I were store pig buying at Lichfield market in early June. In one of the pig pens was a nice Wessex saddleback sow up for auction to be sold as in pig to a Wessex boar. I was really taken with her; she looked in beautiful condition, a nice long well set-up sort of pig. There were the pedigree registration number shapes cut in the edge of her ears, so she must have been a pure breed pig. Dad could see I was very interested in her and he liked the look of her as well although it was not our usual type of pig. Most of our breeding sows had come from the store pigs bought for fattening. As they got to slaughter weight, if there was a good long gilt among them occasionally she would be kept and later put in pig.

Except for me there didn't seem to be much interest in the sow so it was agreed I should have a bid for her. A limit of twenty quid was put on the bidding which I thought wouldn't be nearly enough to buy her. In the end it turned out to be more than enough as I got her for eighteen. The pig breeder who had put her in the sale was not very happy with the price she fetched and made it plain I wasn't going to get the pedigree papers for that money. He should have known if you want a certain price in an auction you put a reserve on it.

Four pens of store pigs were bought, twenty-one pigs in all to complete the day's trading. They all got marked HP on their backs with grease paint and left for Watts to bring to us.

Bill was now keen to own a horse and was saving his money to get one. He subsequently got one off Horace Cox, a horse dealer and blacksmith who had a yard on Darlaston Green. Bill had got in with him one evening when he came to our farm with a heavy horse and cart to fetch our old pig food boiler for scrap. Bill became very friendly with old Horace and bought a piebald colt off him of about eleven hands. The colt was only three years old and had not been broken in to drive. There were plenty of old harness in the barn; people who had turned their horses in the field had just left them when they had got rid of their animals as nobody wanted harness anymore. A gig was acquired free from Dad's friend Percy Haynes, since like the harnesses, nobody wanted them anymore as cars were the thing now.

The colt was named Andy and was gently broken in by Bill with advice from Horace and after a month or so he was being driven around the farm. Mind you, Bill could and still can get animals to do anything; they seem to have confidence in him. This was the start for Bill and he would never be without horses for the rest of his life. A couple of years later Old Horace taught him how to shoe them and Bill would help him in his forge. One of my favourite pictures of him is a full page photo of him in *The Wolverhampton Chronicle* shoeing a horse at Horace's forge in Darlaston.

The Wessex sow we bought from Lichfield Market farrowed nine piglets in the middle of July. They were a lovely litter of pigs and Dad said we should enter them for Brewood Show to be held August Bank Holiday. The entry forms where sent for and filled in for sow and litter; litters must be at least eight piglets and be no more than eight weeks old. Of course, as soon as we had sent the entry form back the sow lay on one of the good piglets and killed it. We were now left with the runt of the litter to make up the eight piglets and our plan had been to leave him at home on the day of the show.

The morning of the show day we did an early milking and pig feeding. I had washed the sow down the night before and put plenty of straw down to keep her and the piglets clean. The sow was loaded into a pig crate and put in the van with the litter one side of the crate and Bill and me the other side. One of the Sunday morning gang was in the passenger seat but I can't remember who it was.

There were seven entries in the sow and litter class and some nice animals amongst them, but even with the runt I still fancied my chances of getting in the prizes. The judges togged up in their white smocks took some time to-ing and fro-ing around the pens and there was another ten minutes of great intensity while they compared their notes before they started to hang the prizes on the pens. First prize went to a Berkshire sow with a litter of eight and well deserved. Second went to a large white sow with ten piglets, then to our surprise we got third with the Wessex sow and litter. We were more than pleased and to celebrate Dad even splashed out on a sausage roll and a bottle of pop for each of us. I don't know where the firm who were doing the catering got their sausage from and I know meat was still rationed, but there was probably more meat in an arrowroot biscuit than there was in them alleged sausage rolls!

Work had now started down in the corner of our bottom field. A firm called Hussey Egan and Pickmore were laying a large sewer pipe. It had been laid all down Bentley and was going along the bottom of the field and through Pleck Park. Our Fanny was spending a lot of her time down by the workings; she would tog herself up before she went down there. It took us a while to find out what she was up to; she was making 'sheep's eyes' at the young chap who was driving the little crane. Blondie was his name, well that's what everyone called him and they soon became great friends but Fanny swore Bill and me to secrecy as she didn't want Dad to find out about it. The secret worked well for me and Bill, as they say knowledge is power so we could use it to blackmail Fanny into doing what we wanted.

No one wanted the pears this year, anyone who did just helped themselves to what they wanted. A few apples were saved but that was about all. The old 'dig for victory' and 'lend a hand on the land' slogans had all been forgotten now.

Things were going along well; me having a punch-up with Fanny most days and Bill with his horse and gig and Bob the collie. Bill now also had a new friend following him – a little heifer calf Bill named Daisy. In the last couple of years it had been the practice to send all our calves to the market but Bill had taken a fancy to this one so it was kept.

Dad now had a new lady friend, Margaret a divorcee, who had come back to live with her parents in a house in Gower Street. Fanny was a bit worried as it looked like things were starting to get serious and I don't think she fancied her as a stepmother. Dad was taking Margaret to George and Maud's Saturday night soirées and he had not done that with any of his other lady friends.

Margaret came to visit us on most Wednesday nights when Dad usually got the whiskey bottle out and they would vanish up to the posh room. We never ever heard them playing the piano up there, however our Harry was happy, things seemed alright and the world still kept turning.

143

At the end of October we had a cold damp spell and it got on Dad's chest. On the Friday morning Dr Davis paid him a visit. He didn't leave a prescription but told our Fanny to keep him warm and give him hot drinks. At about eleven o'clock I was cleaning the pigsties out when Fanny came running down the yard calling 'Dad wants to see you' so I went with her. When we got up to his bedroom he was sitting bolt upright staring at the wall and you could see that he was not breathing. We both knew he was probably dead, so we gently laid him back down on the bed.

Fanny went on her bike to get Dr Davis. As soon as she got there and told him she thought Dad was dead, the first words out of his mouth were 'yes I thought he would be.'

Bill, Fanny and I didn't know what to do next so it was agreed that Fanny would go and fetch Mrs Plant. She was a great help and laid Dad out and did all the necessary things for us. Reg came in the afternoon and he was also a great help. He took Fanny round in the van to tell Dad's brother George and Mini Slater, Jeff's wife leaving them to tell the rest of the family of Dad's death.

Dr Davis came round at about five o'clock to confirm the death; bronchitis was the cause of it. He was surprised to find him all laid out and ready for the undertaker.

Jeff Slater came at half past six, I had fed the pigs and most of the milking had been done by then. With the weekend here there was little that could be sorted out till Monday. Fanny and Aunty Dora, one of Dad's sisters went down to Ennals the undertakers on Saturday morning; they were the firm who also buried Mother. Arrangements were made for the funeral to take place on Tuesday morning, the eighth of November at ten o'clock. Ennals would fetch the body on Monday morning.

We were all in a state of shock, but what could we do; the animals had to be fed and milked so we just had to get on with it. Over the weekend all Dad's brothers and sisters paid us a visit with the exception of his sister Nellie, but she and her husband Percy lived in Northampton. Margaret the lady friend was conspicuous by her absence – she never came and we never saw her again.

The Saturday was the fifth, Bonfire night and Bill and I with some of our friends had built a bonfire in the old sandpit. We should have cancelled it, but our friends were going to have it so Bill and I went to it. Fanny was incensed telling us we should jump in the bonfire because we were going to burn in hell for it anyway.

A lot of people came on Sunday; Jeff, Busty and Aunty Sarah came for most of the day, but tomorrow was a working day so they had all gone by six o'clock in the evening.

The night was a bit difficult with us three on our own and Dad lying dead in his bedroom. Fanny in praying mode didn't help so it was a relief when Ennals fetched him on Monday morning.

On the Monday afternoon Aunty Sarah came and took Fanny out to get her togged up for the funeral. Bill and I were left for Aunty Dora to sort out. I was alright as the suit and clothes Dad had for Mother's funeral fitted me well, so I would wear them. Bill was dragged off to the Co-Op in the town to be rigged out in a new jacket and trousers although he would have been happy to go in his old army surplus clothes.

After all the visitors had gone and the milking and feeding done we held a meeting to decide what we should do. I reckoned we should call it a day and sell-up, but Bill and Fanny wanted to keep the farm going. Fanny said that if we gave the farm up we would be orphans and put in a home. She claimed that we were just the sort of inmates the orphanages were looking for these days and kids like us who were in orphanages were being sent all over the empire by the authorities to use as cheap labour. She had learned about all this when she had been going to the church with Granny. 'Children for the Empire' it was called and we could find ourselves in Canada, Australia or anywhere. That made up our minds – we would dig our heals in. We were staying here!

It was a race on Tuesday morning to get everything fed and milked, but we were ready for the funeral by ten. All Dad's brothers and sisters were there along with most of our older cousins. It was two of these, Jeff and Austin who did the ushering on the day. There were four car loads of us to go to Ryecroft cemetery for the burial. Dad was buried with Mother; his three brothers and Jeff carried his coffin from the chapel down to the grave.

All the family came back to the farm afterwards and the lady who came in to do the cleaning had made a couple of pots of tea. Mother's fancy crockery had been laid out for the occasion as well. This was probably the first time it had seen the light of day as I had never seen it used before. The whiskey stock had been found and

145

Butlers had delivered a new crate of beer last Thursday so we were alright for refreshments.

They all sat themselves round the large living room table and we three kids were brought in for questioning. Haden and Strettons, Dad's solicitors had been contacted and as far as they knew there was no will. There seemed to be some consternation when I said we kids intended staying and keeping the farm going. Uncle Albert said we couldn't and would have to sell up, explaining the reasons why we must leave the farm; the main argument was that we were only children. Most of the others agreed with him but I insisted we were staying.

Austin reckoned we could stay if there were two executors appointed to oversee us. Albert was dead against this and told Austin he was talking through his hat but Austin persisted it was right; if we wanted to stay he didn't see why not and he would be one of the executors. Aunty Dora said she would be the other one but Albert said she was being ridiculous and talked her out of it so Jeff Slater stepped in and said he would do it.

By about two o'clock most of them had gone home and Uncle Albert had taken the pendulum clock off the wall with him. He reckoned it was his and had only been loaned to us although it had been on that wall as long as I could remember. That was the last we ever saw of Uncle Albert and though he used to come to the farm two or three times a week while Dad was alive, he never came again.

Jeff and Austin stayed to sort out the papers in the cupboard and to decide what to do next; Austin would contact the solicitor and do the admin and Jeff would oversee our day-to-day workings.

We kids got on with the running of the farm and Reg Noakes would come and give us a hand most afternoons. Jeff came in the evenings after he had finished work just to check things were going alright and to collect any correspondence for Austin to deal with. Things where now a lot different without Dad but I was doing alright with the pigs and Bill with the cows and at least we were making a go of it.

One morning, about the end of November 1949, a man appeared in the farmyard and announced he was a Council Welfare Officer. He questioned us all in turn as to how old we were and who was living with us. When he found that we lived on our own and as the eldest I was only sixteen years old, he said the Council would not allow this situation to continue. There must be an adult living here as we were only minors and we should be in care.

We explained that Jeff and Austin were looking after us and he took details and their home addresses. When Jeff came that evening we told him all that had gone on but he told us not to worry as he and Austin would sort something out. The outcome was that we had to have someone of adult age (i.e. over twenty-one years of age) living with us. Granny Mac was the obvious person to ask but when she was suggested our Fanny went berserk. Fanny was dead against Granny ever coming back and the venom of her outburst surprised us all.

I remember her supporting Dad when he threw Granny out but I thought after all the God bothering they did together and the circumstances we were in she would have looked a bit more kindly on the idea of Granny living with us again. Jeff and Austin tried to talk her round to the idea but Fanny dug her heals in so we had to look elsewhere.

Harry Bagnal paid us a visit on the Saturday morning and suggested his sister who lived in lodgings would jump at the chance to come and live with us, especially if it was rent free. She lodged near us in St John's Road, so when Jeff came in the afternoon he went to see her. She was only too happy to accept Jeff's offer of free accommodation and arrangements were made to pick her and her bags up with the van in the morning.

I went with Jeff to fetch her on the Sunday morning and as soon as I saw her I knew it was a mistake. This was confirmed by the glee on the faces of the people she had been living with at the thought of getting rid of her.

She was a spinster of about sixty years old in a long black dress with a lace collar and her hair done up in a bun. We got her to the farm and introduced her to Bill and Fanny but I could see by the look on Fanny's face she was not a happy bunny. She got Fanny's goat even further when she announced that we must address her as Miss Bagnal. Her next move was to inspect all the bedrooms and the beds. She decided she was having the posh room as her boudoir and instructed Bill and me to fetch a bed out of the back room and put it in there. By the time Miss had moved her stuff into the room, Fanny had done lunch and Miss inspected our hands to see if we had washed them before we ate it.

It was made plain to us that we were only children and we would do as we were told. She had been put in charge of us and it was for our own good.

After lunch Bill and I made good our escape into the yard and left Fanny to deal with her. We spent the afternoon in the park playing football with our mates until it was milking time. After milking and cleaning up we went in for our tea. Miss had it all laid out for us and she had even made a jam tart although we found out later that Fanny had made it and got the tea on – it seems Miss had the idea she was only there to direct operations.

All of us had to have a wash before tea and our table manners checked while we ate it. Miss then informed us that we would be allowed to listen to the wireless until nine o'clock and bed time would be at nine thirty. That was alright with us as we usually went about that time in the winter.

Miss was up and banging on our bedroom doors at six thirty on Monday morning trying to get us up. We tried to explain to her that it was a waste of time getting up at that time in the winter as we couldn't do anything until it was daylight.

Breakfast was taken in silence as we expected to be put on parade at any moment and inspected to see if we had washed behind our ears. Bill and I were out of the house most of the day so we only had to suffer Miss Bagnal at mealtimes; however Fanny was stuck with her all day. During the day the council welfare man came back on a spying mission but seemed happy that we now had an adult living with us. We got through the day and were even allowed to listen to *Dick Barton Special Agent* on the wireless after tea. It seems Miss had noted our concerns about early mornings, as reveille was at seven thirty on Tuesday morning.

After feeding and milking, Bill and I put some barbed wire in the van and drove it over the fields to repair the fence by Darlaston Road. When we got back to the farmyard at about eleven o'clock, Miss was standing outside the kitchen door in tears with her portmanteau by her side packed. 'I am not stopping here a minute longer,' she announced, 'I've never been so insulted in my life.' I know I shouldn't have done what I did next as I didn't have a driving licence but the journey was only about half a mile and I wasn't going to miss the opportunity; I chucked her bags in the van and took her back to St John's Road as quick as I could.

We never found out what Fanny had said to her to get her into that state but we were all glad to see the back of her.

Jeff was not very happy when he came that evening and found she was gone. We had to find someone else to live with us to keep the council happy and keep the farm. Jeff said he knew a couple who were looking for somewhere to live. One of the men he worked with had his son and new wife living with him. He was recently demobbed and married to a German girl.

Jeff took the van with him when he went home and use it to bring them and their bags tomorrow night all being well.

Fanny took advantage of Miss's demise and soon moved her goods and chattels into the posh room which was to be her boudoir now.

Sure enough, Jeff came the following evening at about seven o'clock with our new lodgers. We kids took to them right away. They were both in their twenties; he was named Fred and his wife was Brigitte and they both worked at the Chance Glass factory in West Bromwich. Jeff gave them a tour of the bedrooms by candlelight for them to pick one they liked. Fred and Brigitte would have liked one of the four poster beds but they hadn't been used for years so the mattresses were a bit grotty.

The middle room on the first floor was chosen as it had a double bed and a fire grate as well. Fanny gave Brigitte some of our bacon and a couple of eggs to cook for their supper. They were both in bed by ten o'clock as they were at work tomorrow and needed to catch three buses to get there. However, we never did see a lot of them as they spent most of their spare time with their friends at West Bromwich. They only slept at the farm but that took care of the need for adults to live with us rule, so everyone was happy.

Chapter Twenty-Three

Before we knew it Christmas was here but we had all been too busy to make any preparations for it. The farm was running to plan and that was the main thing, although having no one that could drive the van was our chief problem. We had to rely on Reg when he came in the afternoons to do any driving.

Collecting pig food from the houses had been abandoned. The only waste we collected now was from Ansell Jones' canteen and the kitchen of a transport café that had opened on the Pleck Road. Waste from the Walsall Co-Op bakery was still collected but we had to give up the one at Cannock.

The Christmas dinner chickens were delivered as most had been ordered before Dad's death. There was a lot of disappointment as they didn't get any pork this year, but we wouldn't be getting any either. A nice big Light Sussex cockerel was saved for our Christmas dinner so we wouldn't go short.

Santa didn't come to Fanny or me this year, only to Bill. He got a new racing bike with a three-speed hub. Fanny, his twin sister had bought it for him from Keys in Walsall. That was the only present given, I didn't give any and neither did Bill. The consequences of Fanny's generous gift would be realised by the end of January.

I didn't feed the pigs till after ten o'clock on Christmas morning as they would only get one good feed to last them the day. The cows were milked at the usual time and they would have to be milked again after tea.

Christmas lunch went well; a good feed was had of the chicken along with the vegetables although pudding was off the menu since we didn't have one anyway.

Our 'pièce de résistance' was a cake made of ice-cream for our tea. It had been ordered a month ago at great cost, five bob from Seagraves' shop. The problem was that Seagraves were closing their shop at twelve thirty on Christmas Day so we had to collect the cake before they closed. We didn't have a fridge so we had to put it in the dairy in a bucket of cold water. By the time the milking had been done and we were ready for tea it had all melted. Fanny found a tin of peaches in Mother's old store – they must have been ten years old, but they seemed alright; there was no smell when we opened them and they tasted alright. So we filled our dishes with them, tipped the melted ice-cream cake on top and got them down us.

Jeff had brought us a large fruit cake his wife had made so we scoffed half of that as well and all had bellies like 'poisoned pups' afterwards.

Some of our friends came after tea along with Fanny's boyfriend Blondie. Jeff had given us a couple of bottles of pop and a bottle of something fancy. 'Westminster cocktail' I think it was called, the bottle looked good with a posh label and gold foil on the top. The stuff in it was a milky colour and tasted nice. With a bottle this posh it didn't take much to convince ourselves it was probably what all the Nobs in the West End were drinking this Christmas.

There were eight of us so we didn't get much each to drink and it wasn't very strong, but we kidded ourselves it was. The gramophone was got going and we played some party games so we had a few hours of fun on what was a sad Christmas.

All our friends had gone home by nine thirty and Fred and Brigitte were at Fred's mother's house for Christmas. They wouldn't be back here until the evening of Boxing Day.

The Postman started bringing all the bills due for payment on the New Year. One of them was a bill from Doctor Davis for twenty-four guineas for treating Dad. When it was queried by Austin, Doctor Davis claimed Dad had never registered with him as a National Health patient and had been treated privately. Everyone thought the bill a bit excessive but Davis was a big noise in the B.M.A., the President or something like that, and must have thought he could charge London prices in Walsall. It had to be paid; there was no way round it.

All the cheques for the big bills were signed by Austin and Jeff and when I asked why I couldn't sign as well I was told I wasn't old enough to be accepted by Lloyds Bank. We had been alright for cash as Dad had a couple of hundred quid in his wallet when he died. Jeff had taken charge of it and would leave us ten quid each week to use as running expenses. We took a few bob off passing customers as well for eggs, chickens, bags of hay, barrows of muck etc., so we did alright. It was the everyday bills that got missed like the baker and the newspapers. Scribbens didn't deliver our bread anymore or York's the newsagents our newspapers. Jeff had stopped them because our Fanny didn't pay their bills – the money she was given to pay for the bread and papers she spent on other things. We were left to go and fetch bread and pay for it as and when we needed it, but we existed mainly on what we bought from the Co-Op bakery when we cleared the waste out.

Our groceries that were still on ration were fetched from Coopers shop on a Friday by Fanny. Things that were strictly rationed like butter and tea she would give away to her friends on her way home. She must have thought she was Queen Victoria distributing largesse to the poor, but it was me and Bill going short. After Fanny had pulled this trick on a couple of occasions Bill or me would accompany her to Cooper's and back home. That didn't work either as the things vanished from the house later.

There were no trips to the Rollerdrome this winter and we didn't get to the pictures much either. Most Saturday nights we would play snooker with our friends; Tucker Salt had a half sized snooker table and he would bring it to the farm with the help of some friends. We would put it on the large table in the kitchen and sort ourselves out into two teams of four players. There was only one cue to play with between all of us, but we managed alright. Most of the arguments were over the scoring, putting too many points on the scoreboard or forgetting to put any on at all. This resulted in the famous plea from Scally Plant of 'if you are going to cheat, cheat fairly'. Some happy hours were had but as the days drew out and the nights got lighter we found other things to do.

The farm seemed to be going along alright – Bill and I thought we were doing OK. One of the problems that worried me was how were we going to replace the pigs that had gone to the butchers. The sows (we had four in all) wouldn't breed enough to keep us going. We needed to buy in store pigs and I didn't have any way of doing this as I had no access to the money. Jeff and Austin had full-time jobs so they couldn't be expected to go to the Auctions and bid. I even went to see Haden and Strettons the farm's solicitors, who according to Jeff were directing operations, to ask if I could buy pigs. They were no help, we were only children and we should be content that our interests were being looked after by our elders and alleged betters, was their attitude. After my meeting with them I had the impression that we kids were not being told about all that was going on, they knew something we didn't. I could feel it in my water.

Towards the end of January, Fred and Brigitte told us they had found a place to live much nearer to their works and would be leaving at the weekend. There would be no problem with this as Jeff already had another couple lined up to move in. They were from West Bromwich as well but worked in Wednesbury so only needed to catch one bus to get there. Jack and Rose were their names and Rose was expecting a baby later in the year. As Fred and Brigitte moved out they moved in and we liked them straight away, even Fanny got on well with them. Unlike the last couple they lived at the farm most of the time except Sunday afternoons when they would usually go and visit their parents in West Bromwich. On occasions if the weather was nice, Bill would take them there in his pony and trap just to give his horse a run out. As Bill had to be back for the milking at about six o'clock Jack and Rose usually came back on the bus.

In the middle of January a man came into the yard looking for a Mrs Power. I explained to him that Mother had passed away over two years ago. He didn't believe me as she had purchased a bike from Keys last Christmas and it then dawned on me it was Fanny he was after. I had a look in the house but she was nowhere to be found, she was probably down the field blowing kisses at Blondie. The man then said he wasn't leaving without some money or Bill's new bike. When I asked why he got a bit 'shirty' with me, I found that the bike had been bought on the 'glad and sorry'. The terms had been five bob deposit and five bob a week for forty-eight weeks. Nothing had been paid since the deposit so there was one pound ten shillings outstanding and he wanted either the money or the bike. I gave him the thirty bob, which bucked him up no end and as I didn't have the payment card he gave me a receipt for it.

Both Bill and I tackled Fanny about it when she came back and she claimed it wasn't her responsibility to pay the five bob a week. She had only paid the deposit for Bill's present so it was up to Bill to pay the five bob a week. Fanny was very contrite for not mentioning to Bill that he was supposed to pay for it, it must have been the excitement of Christmas that caused her to forget. Jeff had the receipt off me and gave it to Austin who must have gone to Keys and settled the bill because we heard no more about it.

Things in the house where now starting to fall apart; Fanny was doing nothing, not even a bit of cooking. If you wanted anything hot you cooked it yourself so I got quite good at knocking up a bit of stew for myself. I even did some pastry with the help of Mother's old Be-Ro pastry book. We did alright for sausage and things like that as Jeff would bring us some from work two or three times a week. Our bacon in the cellar would last a while yet but when that had gone we would have to start collecting our meat ration again.

My barnies with our Fanny were on a daily basis now and we didn't get along at all; mind you we were never great friends. It was after one big punch-up just before my birthday that upset me. Before I went to bed most nights, I would take the box with the watch Granny Mac had given me down from the cupboard and just check it was OK. The evening after the punch up I took it down to have a look and it had been smashed to pieces and put back in the box. You could see someone had taken a hammer to it and it could only have been Fanny's work, but of course I couldn't prove it.

My seventeenth birthday arrived and I decided to treat myself with money I had saved since Christmas. Tucker Salt's brother, Mickey, had a 1935 250cc Triumph motorbike for sale. Mickey wanted twenty quid for it but after a bit of wrangling and playing hard to get, it was mine for eighteen. It was already taxed and insured but I had to go to Harry Webb's the insurance agent to change the insurance over to me and that cost a pound.

I got my provisional licence from the Town Hall; I was old enough to learn to drive the van now as well.

Later in the day as we were getting the cows in for milking I saw Granny Mac by the park fence. She had been to the house but Fanny had sent her away. Granny had a birthday card and a cake she had made for me. She told me that she was coming to live on the other side of the park in Slaney Road as a live-in companion to old lady.

Chapter Twenty-Four

As we got into spring the builders doing the new houses on the allotments started marking out on the top field. When I went to ask them what they were doing I was told that we had been informed last year that they would be starting to build there. It was the first we kids knew about it, but with all the building on the old tip and the allotments it seemed inevitable they would be building on the farm sooner rather than later.

When Jeff came that evening I asked him about it. He took the 'funny you should mention that' sort of attitude to my question; all he knew about it was what the solicitors Haden and Strettons had told him. They had received a notice to quit the farm on Lady Day, March the 25th 1950 and we were to be out by Michelmas Day, September the 23rd.

Our concern now was where we three kids were going to live, but according to Jeff this hadn't been decided yet.

A lot of things came to light now that we had not known before; like the fact that the farm would be built on and that a tentative agreement had already been made with the Council about it. An alternative place would be offered to allow Dad to continue farming but of course this wouldn't apply now. Jeff and Austin reckoned with us kids being minors the Council were making hay while the sun shone.

Another alternative was that Dad would go back to butchering and in fact he had mentioned this early last year when he had the old laundry shop on the corner of Dora and Berkley Streets in mind. At the time we had all dismissed it as just a pipe dream and never took him seriously.

It was a couple of weeks before we found where we were going to live after we left the farm. The Council would find us a three-bedroomed house to move into. It seems we could live in a council house on our own without an adult, but we couldn't live in the farm without one. It struck me as being funny but I thought it wise to keep quiet and not question it.

It would be a while yet before we left and we may have been short on our stock of pigs but it would be about August before the last of the last of them went to the butcher and we still had all the cows.

The sewer being put down by the firm Blondie worked for had been laid under the Darlaston Road now and had reached the edge of our field. They had chopped down the row of pollard willow trees that ran along the brook that fed our pool. They stopped at our fence as the pool would have to be drained before they could continue across Pleck Park.

The basket maker who worked in the old toll house at the bottom of James Bridge was not very happy about that. He had harvested the withies to make his baskets in the past.

I now had my provisional licence to drive the van and was doing the driving to collect the goods we needed. With Reg accompanying me and my L-plates on, of course I was king of the road! I had driven it round the yard and field before but driving on the road took more care.

I had ridden my motorbike on the road but not a lot as I didn't have the time. Sunday afternoon was my motorbike riding time, but then I didn't get very far. It was on one of these trips that Harry Titleys' brother, Gordon, asked me to give him a ride as my pillion. I took my L-plates off and we went up to Barr Beacon. On the way back we were just passing the George Public House in Wallows Lane when the traffic cops in their old Rover car stopped me. Of course they wanted my details and I didn't have them with me. They followed me back to the farm to check my documents and when they found I only had a provisional licence and had no L-plates on, it made their day. Neither of them said anything, they just got in their car and drove off. It was a couple of weeks later that I got the summons to go to court. I was fined two pounds for riding a motor bike without L-plates and according to our Fanny I had joined the criminal classes as well.

On a couple of occasions after tea I visited Granny Mac in Slaney Road but I soon decided it would be better to meet her in the park.

The old dear she was living with had grand ideas and was living in the past. In fact the first words she said to me when I first met her was, 'we used to have servants you know.' She must have thought I was one of them because it wasn't long before she had me working in the garden. She caught me on this hop twice, with me working and she standing there directing operations, so I arranged with Granny to meet her in the park in future. I was surprised that Granny stayed with the old dear as she must have kept her busy, she was a demanding old bugger but I suppose it was somewhere for her to live.

Once the word got around that the farm was finishing we started to get the occasional dealer showing up. They must have thought Bill and I would be easy meat to deal with but we had nothing for sale anyway. All the store pigs would go for slaughter and the four sows to Jeff's mate who would have them for his black market bacon customer. The two boars we had were already spoken for as they were very successful breeders. There would be no problem getting rid of the cows, Sid Evans and Jack Yates had expressed an interest in buying most of them.

We didn't have many fowl left after the Christmas dinner orders had been taken care of and in the spring we had lost a few to foxes. I reckon we had lost some more to two-legged foxes, but we still had enough to keep us in a few eggs. They wouldn't be replaced as we didn't have the usual hundred-day-old chicks as in previous years, anyway we would be here for another couple of months yet.

By mid summer most of the pigs had gone so we had less work to do. I thought I was going to get out on my motorbike a lot more but it was not to be as I couldn't get it to start anymore. All the experts, including Blondie, had a go at it without any success, so in the end I took it to a motorbike repair shop in Stafford Street. They soon got it running again but told me someone had put sugar in my petrol tank and that was the reason it wouldn't start; I wonder who could have done that?

I was now found a job – I didn't really want one as we still had most of the cows and some of the pigs, but in was an offer Jeff said I should take. It happened one morning when a chap come flying into our yard in a car. He announced that Horace Cox had sent him and he was looking to buy equipment to start pig farming. He was interested in buying our boiler and the boshes we cooked the swill in. A pig man would also be needed and I could have the job if I wanted it. He would come back tomorrow to finalise the deal for the boiler and the boshes and I was to see Jeff tonight to agree a price for them.

When Jeff came after tea I told him of the offer to buy all our pig swill cooking stuff. Jeff said he had already seen Horace Slater, his uncle, about what it all would be worth and Horace reckoned about two hundred and twenty quid. That was for the boiler, the four boshes wouldn't be worth much if anything at all. Two of them were old water tanks and two of them were old ammunition barrels from the first world war and they would probably just break-up if you tried to move them. We agreed to ask two hundred and fifty pounds for the boiler – that price would give us plenty of room to haggle. The boshes would go with it as part of the deal. Jeff's view of the job offer was that I could give it a try and pack it up if I didn't like it.

True to his word the chap rolled up again at about eleven o'clock the next morning. I told him what we thought the boiler was worth and he didn't argue and wrote out a cheque for two hundred and fifty quid there and then. If I had the time to spare he would now take me and show me what he was planning to do. Well, I could find time, couldn't I? If it was just to get a ride in his posh car.

While we were in the car he told me that he had just taken over the running of the family business which was a chain of hardware shops around the Walsall area. He was only in his mid twenties and had done his National Service in the R.A.F. and was determined he was not going into the forces again. The Korean War had started a few weeks ago and he saw that as the start of world war three. According to him this was the Russians starting to take over the world and this couldn't be allowed as that was a job the Americans had set their heart on. Before long they would be calling the likes of him up again for the forces. There was still only two ways of dodging the draft, farming or coal mining, so he was going to be a farmer. Well you could see he certainly wasn't cut out to be a collier.

We got to his house; it was on the opposite side of Walsall to the farm, about a four mile run. It was a large modern house with a four acre garden all nicely kept. He wasn't married and lived there with his mother and his sister. I was taken through the garden to a patch of scrub land he had bought and this was where he was going to start his farm. The next half an hour was spent with him explaining his plans for the farm. He had ordered some pre-cast concrete pig sties but these had not been delivered yet. I suggested he would be better with some pig arks and some sheep wire fencing. If the pigs were loose on the land it would help to clear it. But this wouldn't do, he must have proper sties for his sows to farrow in as this was the advice of the experts he had consulted. The farm would breed all its own pigs and the plans were to start by purchasing some in-pig sows. It seems he was determined to do it the hard way, he had read all the books of course and now knew it all. After he had explained all his grand plans to me I was introduced to his mother; she seemed a nice old dear, as was his sister who was married. Her husband also worked for the family firm. I was then taken back to the farm and told he would come and see me again after his concrete sties had been delivered. It would probably be another fortnight before he could have the boiler as we still had the boars and sows to feed.

Bill was still milking five cows, they were the ones Jack Evans and Sid Yates were going to have. The other five had been sold to a dealer who came in the yard one evening. Bill did a deal with him for the remaining cows and when Jeff came later he thought it a good one. It wasn't top whack but if they had gone to auction they wouldn't have made much more, in fact with the cost of the transport to get them there and the auctioneer's commission we may have received a lot less.

There had been a lot fewer working horses turned out for grazing this year. Working horses were vanishing off the roads at an ever increasing rate now. We still had the old Walwoods' mare and Sid Perrins' pony in the field along with a couple of riding ponies. One of them was a red roan one and belonged to Margaret the daughter of a publican who kept a pub at Wood Green. Margaret and I became very friendly and I had ambitions to one day take her up into the hay loft and show her the owls' nest.

My chance to impress her came one Sunday when her horse got in the river. This was the River Tame which flowed under the bottom of James Bridge and across the corner of our field and under the railway. It wasn't very deep at only about three feet normally, but it was filthy with industrial waste and fast flowing. In fact where it ran past F. H. Loyds they had built a little Hydro electric station on it.

Between James Bridge and the railway, the sides of it had been banked, probably to stop it flooding onto the field and the horse must have got on top of the bank and slipped down into it. I collected Bill and we went down there taking a length of rope with us. When we got there the animal seemed alright and didn't seem injured in any way and was quite calm. We got the rope on its head collar and walked the horse along the river towards the railway bridge where the bank wasn't so steep. With a bit of kidding and us pulling on the rope the horse managed to scramble back up the bank. Its legs and belly where a bit oily and smelly but otherwise he didn't seem any worse for his little adventure.

When Margaret came in the afternoon I thought I could play the hero but it didn't work; she was giving Bill the 'glad eye' not me.

It was August by now and most of the animals had gone from the farm so the whole place was looking a bit sad. Sid Yates had fetched the three cows he had picked out and Jack Evans was planning to collect his two on Sunday morning. He would walk them up the Broadway to his farm at the Fullbrook. Jack was only a part-time farmer with four or five cows and about a dozen pigs; his full-time job was with the Walsall Council Parks Department.

By the middle of the month we were left with Bill's pony and Daisy the calf, the dogs, cats and half a dozen chickens. One of our main problems was stopping the thieving. Once word had got round that we were leaving the farm it seems we had become open house for the looters. The dairy equipment and things like that had been sold, but we still had a lot of small things like wheelbarrows and general farming tools. I would have liked to collect them up and take them to Lichfield market but we had no one to take them, so most of them got stolen. One or two bits of Mother's old jewellery that now belonged to our Fanny vanished as well. A little gold watch like a locket on a neck chain was probably the most valuable piece to vanish. Our lodgers, Jack and Rose were so concerned that they put a padlock on their bedroom door and locked it before going off to work.

We had a nasty incident one Saturday afternoon that has always stuck in my mind. Bill and I were down the yard talking to our Uncle George when Fanny came running down to tell us someone was in the top bedrooms banging. When we all got up there it was a man helping himself to the floor boards. Its was a good job we had Uncle George with us because he got a bit nasty when we asked him what he was up to. His argument was they were going to knock the place down so he may as well have the floor boards. George got him out of the house but he took the few boards he had got up with him.

About the only thing we made a few bob on were the pigsty roofs, they had been gas-tarred every year and were in good condition. Reg had the pick of them as he was building some pigsties in Palfrey. Now we were finishing here Reg was going to keep pigs himself. One of his milk customers had a large garden with some spare land at the bottom and would rent it out to him. The way Reggie Noakes had helped us since Dad died, he could have anything he wanted off us free. Most of it was bought by Mr Thurstance who was building some stables at the end of Slater's Lane. He had to pay for it of course. A few of the sheets and timbers were bought by people who were making themselves garden sheds; they only needed two or three sheets to make a roof.

The large war surplus shed Dad had bought a few years ago to use as a fowl pen was still in good condition. It had been a shame to use it to keep fowl in since we think it may have been used for a shop before we had it. Bill and I gave it a good clean out and scrubbed the floor. Jeff advertised it and someone bought it to use as an office and I think we got as much for it as Dad had bought it for, so everyone was happy.

We had had an offer for our van some time ago from Mr Davis who lived at the bottom of Gower Street. They would take the van as soon as we had finished using it. He and his wife were opening a greengrocer's shop in the old laundry in Dora Street.

Chapter Twenty-Five

Towards the end of August a lorry came to fetch the boiler and tanks. Jeff and Uncle Horace had come and disconnected all the pipework last Sunday. One of our worries was that they would damage the lagging on the boiler when they loaded it on the lorry but it was alright, they had obviously moved boilers before.

Mr Hughes the future pig farmer who had bought them came as they were being loaded. He told me that some of his sties had been delivered and would I like to make a start on putting them together. I had nothing else planned so I promised to go up and make a start next Monday morning.

I arrived there on my motorbike bright and early on the following Monday morning. No one was up out of bed when I got there and the gardener was the first person to show up. He took me in his shed at the bottom of the garden and we sat chatting until about eight thirty when Mr Hughes came down to us. He took me through the gate at the bottom of the garden onto the patch of scrub land where he planned to have his pig farm. A pile of concrete blocks and posts were stacked to one side – these were to be the sties. I was given a plan of how the bits all slotted together, shown where he wanted them erected and just told to get on with it. I pointed out that the posts which the sides slotted into should be cemented into the ground. Just dig them in for the time being was the plan, they would be alright once the floors had been concreted.

The slabs for the sides were heavy to lift into the slots in the posts once they were erected but I just took it steady. There was a tea break twice a day at ten thirty in the morning and at three in the afternoon. At these times the housekeeper would bring a pot of tea and two mugs to the gardener's shed. Tea was still rationed but they seemed to have a supply from somewhere.

On Saturday morning I had almost finished putting up the sties when Hughes came and gave me five pounds, my wages for the week. He told me he would pay me as a casual until he had some pigs and then he would formalise my employment as the pig man with him. At the moment he hadn't ordered any more sties and next week I could start sorting the boiler and swill cooking arrangements.

Talking to him I now got the impression that his urges to be a farmer was cooling off a bit. The Korean War had been going for a couple of months and neither Moscow nor New York had been bombed, so he thought his chances of being called up for military service were lessening by the hour. At twelve thirty I rode off on my motorbike and never went there again, and he never came to ask me why.

I thought about it a lot and I was glad in a way, farming was not what I really wanted to do. I saw the closing of the farm as more of a relief. Bill didn't feel the same; I could see he was very sad at the prospect of us leaving. Fanny never said anything but I think she was happy to see the end of it as well.

During the week a man from the Council Housing Department came to see us because we had been allocated a three-bedroomed house in Alexandra Road. The surprise was that they were dealing directly with us for once and not through a third party. One of us was to go down to the Town Hall on Monday and collect the keys and go and have a look at the house.

Fanny went for the keys and when she came home I took her to the new house on the back of my motorbike. Once we got inside the house it became clear that most of the farmhouse furniture would not fit in there. Fanny had brought a tape measure with her and we took down the size of all the rooms.

The fire grate in the living room still had the cast iron hob with the oven in it and a back boiler for hot water. In the kitchen were an electric stove and a washing boiler built in and a separate bathroom at the end. With a back boiler for hot water, a bathroom and an indoor toilet this would be luxury living for us.

Over the next few days we worked out what we would be taking with us. The suite and carpet from the posh room was the first on the list together with the bedroom suite Mother had bought at the same time. We each picked out a single bed to take and a small chest of drawers. Tables would be our problem as we only had the kitchen and living room tables, one was six foot by four foot and the other one eight foot by four. It was Reg who came up trumps again as he found us a little kitchen table from one of his milk round customers. We swapped them one of our marble wash stands for it.

Fanny now started to put the household things she wanted to take in Granny's old room. This proved to be a mistake as among it was a nice canteen of cutlery in a leather-bound box, and it didn't take long for that to vanish. Like the bits of jewellery that had gone missing it could only have been taken by someone with access to our house, one of our friends perhaps.

Finding new homes for the dogs and cats was our main problem now but Bill would keep his dog Bob. The yard dog Sid Yates would take; he was a big black rough-coated dog Dad had got to replace old Joey when he had to be put down a couple of years ago. He had the very original name of Rover and was let loose to roam the yard at night. In the daytime he was loosed in the corner of the garden on a long chain, with a barrel for his kennel. From this position he could see down the drive that led to the farm and he would certainly let you know if anyone was coming. Sid took Rover (complete with chain and barrel) and we gave him our old twelve-bore shotgun as well.

Nelly was the other dog; she was a stray that had taken up residence in the barn by the farm gate. She had a pup in there in the spring time and Bill used to give her a drop of milk when we had the cows. One of Bill's friends had the pup for a pet and it was nearly fully grown by now. Mr Downs the R.S.P.C.A. inspector came; he had been an old friend of our parents for a long while and he would take Nelly and see if she could be re-homed.

He was a bit concerned about the cats. The she cat that used to have a litter of kittens in the cow shed was fairly tame but the other four were feral. Mrs Perry, who lived in the house next to the farm, used to feed Jacko the she cat and make a fuss of her, so said she would give her a home. Mr Downs would collect the other four, if he could catch them.

Jeff and Austin came one Saturday afternoon and got us all together. They had decided that before we left the farm we should all get togged up with some new clothes. We would be looking for jobs and needed to go for our interviews looking smart, as first impressions count according to Austin. Fanny had bought a few new clothes since Dad's death but Bill and I had worn the stock of army surplus stuff he had bought from Lichfield market. The suit I had worn for the funeral was a bit tight on me now.

When I told Granny of how we were going to be togged out she said I should get a new suit and she knew just the tailor to make it. Later in the week she came to the park railings and told me to be at her lodgings at seven o'clock on Wednesday night. When I got there it was as I had suspected – the tailor was a relative of the old dear she lived with. Like the old dear, he was living in the past and thought that by pricing his suits in guineas it made them look more upmarket. I didn't see it that way – to me it was a ruse to screw an extra eight bob out of me. However, with Granny's prompting I chose a dark blue pin-stripe material for it to be made in. The tailor got his measure out and took my sizes and I was to go back the following Wednesday evening for a fitting. I had the fitting and a week later the suit was ready to try on. Everyone liked it and I must agree the tailor had made a smashing job of it; I was more than pleased so I paid him the eight guineas.

Bill still had his pony and Daisy the calf and he could probably have found a place at Cox's for the pony but they didn't want the calf. Jeff went and saw Percy Haynes and he agreed Bill could turn both his pony and the calf out in one of his fields, but this would only be a temporary measure while Bill found a permanent place for them.

The move to the new home was planned for the following Wednesday. The chap from the Council came to see what furniture we would be taking with us to the house. After an inspection he told us the Council would move it for us. The reason for this offer was that it was coming from a very old property and there was a risk that it may be infected with woodworm. It would have to go in what they called the 'bug wagon' which fumigated the furniture as they transported it.

The workmen came and took it on the afternoon and Fanny and I followed them up to Alexandra Road on my motorbike. Fanny supervised the unloading, telling the men where she wanted the things put. I must say they were very helpful. After the furniture had all been unloaded we opened all of the windows to give the place a blow. It seemed like no one had lived there for a while and the place smelt a bit musty. A couple of hours were spent arranging the things how we wanted them, but after the farmhouse it was like being in a rabbit hutch.

We then locked the place up and went back to the farm. Most of the original furniture in the farmhouse would have to be left like the Victorian monstrosity we called a sideboard. In fact except for the posh room and Mom and Dad's bedroom the rest of the rooms were still fully furnished. Mainly with large pieces of oak cupboards and chests of drawers that were much too large for modern houses.

When Bill came home at about nine o'clock that evening we told him he could move to the new house, but he said he would be staying at the farm. Bill had another surprise for us as well – he had got a job. He would be starting work at Carrington's, working on the drop hammers on Monday morning.

At the weekend Jack and Rose left, they went back to live with Jack's mother at West Bromwich. They had been trying to get a council house ever since we had been given the notice to quit but they were only put on the waiting list.

On the Monday morning the workmen came and took down the iron railing that had separated the farm from the park. A bulldozer followed them and scraped a path from the farm gate up to the railway bridge into the park. This was where Gower Street would extend too in the future. I think the Council were trying to tell us something.

On the Tuesday I packed what bits and pieces I needed in a bag and moved out to the house in Alexandra Road. I never went back to the farm again and had no regrets. The last thing about the place that I always remember was Mother's old bike still propped against the wall where she had left it nearly three years ago.

Fanny followed me in the evening; Blondie brought her on his motorbike. Bill didn't come as he was determined to stick it out to the bitter end at the farm. He eventually rolled up late on Thursday evening. We could see he was very upset, he had been to work and then spent the evening at Cox's. When he had got back to the farm at about nine o'clock, they had taken the roof off and knocked half of it down.

The last three years had been incredible and all of us probably learnt more in that time than we would in the rest of our lives. None of us would ever be lost and we all knew how to hit the ground running.

During the week Fanny had got herself a job at Frosts who had a factory up on Fieldgate. They employed a lot of young girls assembling electrical goods. I had already decided what I was going to do as my call-up papers for National Service would be here in the next six months. That stopped me going back into engineering as I would have to leave again in six months' time. No employer would have you on a training programme for that length of time. Anyway there was a big wide world out there and I wanted to see some of it. If I joined the army as a volunteer I would get some choice of which regiment to join but with the call-up you got put where they wanted more men.

On the following Monday morning I went to the army recruiting office in Queen Street, Wolverhampton. After taking my details they sent me for a medical at an old school at the top of Snow Hill. I was given all the tests including sight and filling the bottle etc. and sent back to the recruiting office. It was there that I was told I had passed the medical A1. No one had said anything at Snow Hill. They had just checked me, grunted and wrote their findings down. I could apply to join any of the regiments except the brigade of guards; I wasn't tall enough for them. Well it had to be the local regiment, the South Staffords, and so that was what I did. A list of what I had to take with me was given; ration book, identity card, medical card, and my toothbrush and razor.

My date for joining was the twenty-seventh of September 1950 at Whittington Barracks, Lichfield. The ten days I had before joining I spent helping on Sid Yates' farm. I even sold my old motorbike to Gordon Johnson, one of his workmen before I went. Anyway I was off on a great adventure and tomorrow would be a brand new day!